God Holds You

A Pandemic Chronicle

SARAH S. SCHERSCHLIGT

This book is dedicated to
Ridgeway, Magdalene and Lydia.
You are my heart.

CONTENTS

FOREWORD

Each summer the Collegeville Institute for Ecumenical and Cultural Research at St. John's University in Minnesota opens its doors to pastors, ministers, lay leaders, and other thinkers for a week-long, intensive workshop in writing. I met Sarah Scherschligt in 2013, when I was teaching at the workshop. She was a joy to work with: intelligent, enthusiastic, continually consulting and collaborating with other pastors.

On her way home from the Institute, Sarah wrote some haikus about me and a few others from the class. Soon this group became the Wholly Writers, women pastors who stayed in close contact from that time on. We've all shared our writing—and our lives—with texts, emails, and Zoom calls.

When Sarah sent her writing to us, she prefaced her work: *I hold you all in my thoughts as we re-enter into pastor/family life and try to keep the spaciousness of our time in Collegeville.* Years later, in COVID-19 times, she wrote to a larger group, her congregation, and then to an even wider Facebook audience. Navigating through an unprecedented global pandemic, each of her "God holds you" posts, numbered in sequence, offered mental, emotional, spiritual help to so many—she has lots of friends!

Sarah's opening words to our group years ago, *I hold you all in my thoughts,* express the all-embracing reach of this new, beautiful book, *God Holds You,* which recreates her original, daily entries. Clarified, comforted, we follow Sarah, joining her in honest deliberations of self, family and friends, religious congregations, our social and historical world. She makes true judgment calls with humor and wisdom.

I love that Scripture comes alive in her book:

June 7, 2020
Day 85

. . . It did my soul well to slip into patterns that are ancient and familiar. I was soothed by the long, repetitive reading of Genesis 1 that I've heard hundreds of times.

It was good. It was good. It was good.

Readers will appreciate getting to know the people who inhabit this book. They become real through description and dialogue, actions and reactions. Sarah's voice, always warm and welcoming, invites us into a variety of scenes and situations. She pays attention, centering on everyone's joys and sorrows, fears and strengths, successes and failures.

We all will get to know more about ourselves reading her book. Grateful for her honesty on failing sometimes as a wife, a mother, a pastor, a leader of racial equity, we'll learn how to ask for forgiveness, how to strive for change, how to be gentle with ourselves and others. How to show empathy.

There will be many Sarah moments we'll want to emulate:

April 27, 2020
Day 44

. . . Zooming down a hill I laughed as I remembered the original meaning of the word "zoom." As my legs struggled to crest that same hill a few minutes later, I felt like a person, not just a face behind a screen. I felt playful, childlike and strong. I felt free. I felt like myself . . .

I miss myself. I miss the balance of all my parts. I was grateful today for fifteen minutes on a bike and the wholeness that came with it.

God Holds You is a wonderful account of survival during a major upheaval in our lives, but it is more than that. It is a powerful meditation on how to live true and free—joyful—in this very challenging world of ours.

—Marge Barrett, March 4, 2022.

Marge Barrett is the author of a memoir, *Called: The Making & Unmaking of a Nun*, and two books of poetry, *My Memoir Dress* and *If You Have Something to Say, Margaret*.

INTRODUCTION

On March 15, 2020, I first typed the words "God holds you." I didn't know I was starting to write a book, but then I also didn't know we were on the cusp of a multi-year pandemic.

That was the first Sunday that the church I serve as a pastor live-streamed worship services because of COVID-19. The virus was so new that everyone was reeling with shock and fear. That evening, after I cuddled my young daughters to sleep, I wrote a brief reflection on Facebook in order to inject a pastoral voice of comfort and stability into a panicking world.

The next night, I wrote another post. Within a few days, I had established a pattern. After my kids were asleep, I would write a reflection, always ending with the phrase, "Sleep well world. God holds you." In the beginning, I thought I would write for a couple of weeks. Instead, I wrote for thirteen months.

I wrote so that the posts would have significance for the day they were written, and no further. They don't describe everything that happened in a day, much less the year. If I had been trying to capture the comprehensive scope of news and emotions in the first year of the pandemic, I may have crafted each post differently. As they are, they are like spiritual journalism, giving real-time insight about faith and life in the exceptional stretch of days from March 15, 2020 to April 5, 2021.

With each post, I tried to bring God's presence to the forefront while also attending to the pandemic reality of the day. I often engaged with scripture; I am a preacher, after all. I was intentional about being first person, speaking only for myself. I was also intentional about focusing primarily on the pandemic, even in the midst of other significant societal, political and personal events.

I typed most of the posts on my phone. This kept them short. When I finished, I posted them on my Facebook page. Every morning, our parish administrator reposted them on our church's website and social media.

I didn't make any effort to get a wider distribution. These were personal and pastoral, written for my people. Some posts received a few likes. Others were shared broadly and garnered scores of comments. A handful of people read them every day and conveyed appreciation for the comfort they brought. In turn, I was grateful for the community that formed around them; the people I connected with through "God Holds You" posts were pandemic lifelines.

When I stopped writing, thirteen months into the pandemic, COVID-19 seemed to be getting under control, at least in Northern Virginia where I live. Vaccines were widely available for people over age eleven, and infection rates were going down.

As of the writing of this introduction, we are twenty-five months in. The pandemic is not over, but it has changed significantly. Widespread vaccines for ages five and up have made it less lethal. We expect a vaccine for kids under five will be announced any day now. New variants keep appearing (Delta in the fall, Omicron in the winter), but we are learning to ride the waves and live fully when and where we can. Scientists' best predictions now say that COVID-19 will be endemic, similar to the flu.

We are all vaccinated in our household. We finally renovated our kitchen and took a trip to Nashville, both of which were postponed in spring of 2020. Church and school meet in person, with masks optional. We still wear masks in crowded places, take the uncomfortable COVID-19 test when we think we're exposed, and live with the uncertainty that any day may mean a new variant or a new quarantine. We continue to adapt. God still holds us.

A year has passed since I wrote my final post. As I gained some distance on these writings, I discovered I wanted them to endure as a complete collection, beyond the flighty realm of digital content, so I compiled them into this book. They have been lightly edited, but essentially they are the original posts.

I hope this book is meaningful for the people of my church, Peace Lutheran in Alexandria, Virginia, as well as the smattering of people who faithfully read the original posts. I will be gratified if it can be a small part of our collective remembering, which is an essential part of our healing.

I'd be thrilled if it were widely read, perhaps used by individuals and groups to reflect on the pandemic. I imagine it sparking questions like, "How did my faith sustain me? Where did I find grace? What was lost and what was gained? In light of the pandemic, how do I want to live now?" I also hope that it will become a useful piece of the historical record, so that decades from now, researchers can use it to understand how people responded to the COVID-19 pandemic.

Above all, I have created this book for my daughters, Magdalene Suzanne and Lydia Sarah Ruth. They were four and three years old when the pandemic hit, and they've now lived nearly half their lives under its shadow. I hope that sometime when they are adults, they will read this book and discover how God's enduring promises got us through this extraordinary time, their own childhood.

—Sarah S. Scherschligt, April 17, 2022. Easter.

SECTION 1

INTO THE WILDERNESS
March 15, 2020 – May 24, 2020

"Then Moses ordered Israel to set out from the Red Sea, and they went into the wilderness." (Exodus 15:22)

~~~

"There are estimates that if nothing goes right and if we fail to flatten the curve and if health systems are overwhelmed, we might see the deaths of as many as a million and a half people in the United States."
—*Francis Collins, Director of the National Institutes of Health, March 14, 2020*[1]

"MARGARET BRENNAN: So millions of children across this country are looking at the possibility of not being able to go to school for at least a few weeks—
DR. FAUCI: Right.
MARGARET BRENNAN: —possibly longer.
DR. FAUCI: Right.
MARGARET BRENNAN: Their parents are going to try to figure out what to do with them.
DR. FAUCI: Right—right."
—*Interview with Dr. Anthony Fauci, March 15, 2020*[2]

March 15, 2020

This thought came to mind as I cuddled my little one to sleep tonight: *God will hold you.*

Suddenly, I barely recognize this world. It's not only because of the virus—though I can hardly go there—but also because of the economy and politics and fear. The suffering is bound to be massive, even if we manage to stop the viral spread. It's like all at once, everything that gave life its basic structure is up for grabs.

Still. I believe God holds us. As foundation and bedrock. As the force that keeps us in place when the world is swirling. As a mother soothes a restless child.

God holds you. May you feel God's arms around you tonight. Sleep well world.

~Pastor Sarah

March 16, 2020
Day 2

The day started with our whole family running across the street in our pajamas. A neighbor was heading out the door to go to work and when we saw her through our picture window, we popped over to check in.

We waved and chatted with more neighbors in one day than we have in a month. All from a distance. But all so sweet.

The day was filled with neighborly kindnesses. A bouquet of daffodils. The offer of a grocery run. At night we read the story of the Good Samaritan, which in our kids' Bible is titled "The Good Neighbor."[3]

Jesus is called Emmanuel, which means "God is with you." I've also heard it translated as "God moves into the neighborhood." I like that. Jesus was in our neighborhood today. I hope he was in yours too.

Sleep well world. God holds you.

March 17, 2020
Day 3

Today I noticed people getting creative. Children's author Mo Willems is giving online doodling lessons. I drew alongside my children, as Mo taught us to create Gerald, the famous elephant of the *Elephant and Piggy* books. That five minutes of concentration calmed my brain. I was oddly proud of what I made. And I was happy.

God created out of dirt. Jesus put mud on a blind man's eyes and recreated his world. Today our kids made mud pies and I planted some zinnia seeds. It was good.

God is in creativity. The songs and art and poetry that come out of this time will be breathtaking. So too, in their ways, will be the government programs and church structures and community connections that recreate people's worlds.

All things will be made new.

Sleep well world. God holds you.

March 18, 2020
Day 4

Grief is starting to settle in. No one I know has died. No one has even gotten sick. But the little losses are piling up like snowflakes on a branch. No playdates. No grocery stop on the way home from work.

I found notes today about the family vacation we were planning for August. Are we still planning it? I grieve for the ability to plan.

There's a church overlooking Jerusalem built in the shape of a teardrop. It's where Jesus wept. What a perfect place for a church. When I envision Jesus crying, I sense great love.

I am going to try to welcome grief as the permanent resident it's bound to become.

I am going to try to trust that when I welcome grief, I also welcome the love that will bear it.

Sleep well world. God holds you.

March 19, 2020
Day 5

Our bishop gathered all our pastors on a Zoom call today. We were approximately sixty people in a massive *Brady Bunch*-style formation. Below each of our faces, our names appeared.

My church pulled together a care team today. These ten people will be the front line of spiritual care for our congregation. We listed all the people we were worried about and assigned them to a team member. There's now a new spreadsheet filled with names.

Jesus changed systems and confronted the powers that held the world captive to sin, yes. But he did it by encountering individual human beings. Relationships. One after another. People with names.

In a time of isolation, I think names become even more important.

Say yours out loud. Say someone else's too. This diminishment will not last forever. You are still connected. You have a name.

"I have called you by name, and you are mine." (Isa 43:1b)

Sleep well world. God holds you.

March 20, 2020
Day 6

Today I presided over a wedding. The original plan was for the father-of-the-bride, who is a pastor, to fly in to officiate at a small ceremony. But he couldn't get here, and even a small ceremony was too big. Instead, I performed the wedding outdoors, six feet from the couple, while the groom's parents held up a phone so the rest of the family could witness it online.

It wasn't ideal. I'm certain the couple was disappointed. But it was also lovely in its simplicity. The thing that mattered most happened; they got married.

After the ceremony we stood on the sidewalk beside the busy road in front of the church with a "Just Married" sign. Passing cars honked and waved with delight. The church members who live across the street pulled out a tambourine and jangled it with joy.

Jesus made sure the wine didn't run out at a wedding party. He knew: celebration is essential. We always have reason to shake that tambourine.

Sleep well world. God holds you.

March 21, 2020
Day 7

I plan to write these reflections every day until the church celebrates Easter. No, not the Easter that's slated to happen in three weeks, but the one where the choir sings shoulder to shoulder, and we dip real bread in a chalice held by human hands, and the passing of the peace takes forever because of all those hugs.

I plan to write until then, except on Saturdays because I need a sabbath. Sabbath is the day set aside each week to cease from work and rest in God's care. Sabbath helps a faithful people remember that we aren't God, and we don't need to act like we are.

Jesus often retreated and took time away for renewal. We can too. Even now. Especially now.

People who regularly keep sabbath know it takes a little planning. You may be thinking, "How's she posting when she says she's taking a sabbath?"

I wrote this yesterday.

Sleep well world. God holds you.

March 22, 2020
Day 8

Am I allowed to say I don't want to be a televangelist? The people of my church—like countless others—have done a heroic job of getting us online. Worship today was lovely, but it wasn't what I wanted.

I poured bleach into the baptismal font to sanitize it. When I reached in for confession, it smelled like a pool. I preached about God setting a table and anointing with oil, but no one ate and no one was anointed. I looked into a camera instead of the eyes of my beloved church.

It was a beautiful service, but I long for real things with real people. That's why we rang the church bell before worship, something we rarely do. The world needs all the real reminders of God's presence we can get. Or at least I do.

Tonight I turned to the book of Lamentations. It begins, "How lonely sits the city that once was full of people." (Lam 1:1) Amen to that. But it ends with a hopeful plea: "Restore us to yourself, oh Lord. That we may be restored." (Lam 5:21) May it be so, Lord. May it be so.

Sleep well world. God holds you.

March 23, 2020
Day 9

Today's announcement of school closures forces a massive recalibration of expectations. This will not end soon. I keep hearing people say, "How will we get through this?" I wish I knew.

At the same time, my kids (ages three and four) are having the time of their lives. They haven't been rushed for a week. They haven't even been in a car. They wake up late and play all day. The surfaces in our house are covered in art projects. Life is slow and full.

When the psalmist told us about our journey through the valley of the shadow of death, he promised goodness in the midst of it.

"You set a table before me in the presence of my enemies." (Ps 23:5)

That's not to say the enemies disappear. Fear and greed and misguided leaders and sickness and despair are present and accounted for. But among them, something else appears.

I don't know any better word for it than grace. It looks like cherry blossoms and smells like kids who have played outside. It sounds like a three-year-old belting *Frozen 2* and tastes like chocolate chip cookies fresh from the oven.

The table has been set. My cup overflows.

Sleep well world. God holds you.

March 24, 2020
Day 10

I heard the phrase "the new normal" at least ten times today, including from my own mouth.

The phrase drives me crazy, but it's true. Today felt . . . normal. Having back-to-back Zoom meetings no longer feels noteworthy. Now it's just what I do.

I didn't worry today that I was getting sick. I didn't obsessively check in on my parents to see if they're OK. Instead of panicking because we're almost out of bananas, I simply added them to the grocery list.

I just lived. And it was boring and really nice.

I have a hard time balancing this sense of calm with the knowledge that there are people losing jobs, falling ill, and sacrificing for the common good. I'm guilty of a kind of spiritual pride that says if I'm not in anguish about the world, I'm not being faithful.

There's blessing to be found in rhythm and routine. Jesus certainly had plenty of days that weren't recorded in scripture, even as he was contending with the powers of the world.

There's no way that this actually is the new normal. But today, I'll take it.

Sleep well world. God holds you.

March 25, 2020
Day 11

A member of our church is a pediatric hospitalist. She reported that a few nights ago, some doctors joined the nurses in their 3:00 a.m. mid-shift huddle and led them in a song. The next night she brought her ukelele, and they did it again.

Why do I love that so much? I think it's because I know how powerfully I experience God by singing with other people. It's healing and catharsis and play and joy. It's worship and prayer. There's nothing else like it.

The apostle Paul wrote, "And sing! Sing your hearts out to God!" (Col 3:16, MSG)

Of all the things I miss about church-as-usual, singing with people is near the top of the list. Zoom is great for meetings, but there's no online platform that enables people to sing together. The time lag makes it impossible.

Maybe that's why I love the idea of those doctors and nurses singing. It's church. Even in the midst of scary and stressful nights, there will be music.*

Sleep well world. God holds you.

The phrase "there will be music" is from one of my favorite poems, "A Brief for the Defense," by Jack Gilbert.[4]

March 26, 2020
Day 12

For the past few years, I've served on the board of the Faith Alliance for Climate Solutions (FACS), most recently as the treasurer. I am passionate about our mission, and I love being part of this organization.

For the past two weeks, I've slipped farther and farther behind in everything. I've cut a lot of fat off my schedule, but still, my totally chaotic in-box has made it clear that something else has to go. In a desperate moment, I sent an email with the subject line "hitting the wall" to the other leaders of FACS.

They received my email with enormous grace. They gave me a two-month hiatus, and other board members have already picked up my duties. I am breathing a sigh of relief.

This is a matter of calling. My calling has just changed because the world has just changed. I now need to be a different kind of parent, a different kind of pastor, and a different kind of daughter. Plus, I need much more reflective time to figure it all out.

When the apostle Paul wrote about spiritual gifts, he described them as spread out in a community: "There are a variety of gifts, but the same spirit." (1 Cor 12:4) No one person is gifted for the complete task.

Tonight I am keenly aware of my own limitations. At the same time, I'm at peace because of the abundance that shows up through the community. One spirit unites us for the common good.

Sleep well world. God holds you.

March 27, 2020
Day 13

Grandparents.

Mine have all been dead for at least a decade, but my kids are lucky to have all four still alive. In normal times, we talk to them a few times a month. In the past two weeks, we've connected with them almost every day, often via FaceTime.

We've had art class with Papa, reading with Grammy, and story & songs with Oma and Grandpa. We have a beloved neighbor we call our bonus grandma. Our kids have played in her yard. She made us playdough. We fetched her milk.

Is it a stretch to say that a silver lining of this virus is that we're relating to each other across generations?

I've been impressed with the way Gen-Zers have self-isolated out of love for their elders, and how the over-seventy set has learned social media. Millennials are calling their older relatives to learn how to knead bread. The wisdom of people who lived through World War II is regarded as invaluable.

I sense that the world we're suddenly living in is similar to my grandparents' Depression-era childhoods. I have thought of them more in the past two weeks than in a decade. I miss them in part for conversations I never knew I'd want to have.

The phrase "from generation to generation" shows up throughout scripture. It indicates that the promise of the future is rooted in the faithfulness of the past. From generation to generation, God is faithful.

Sleep well world. God holds you.

March 30, 2020
Day 16

I have learned that I don't like change, or at least I don't like change that happens quite so relentlessly.

In the Washington, D.C. region, we're once again readjusting our horizons. June 10th. That's the new date when we should expect the lockdown to end. June. Tenth.

The news came today quickly and surprisingly, but not really. Really, it's been months in the making and I could have predicted it. If I had, I'd be prepared. I'd have stocked up on Home Depot-y projects. I'd have learned how to be a worship-tech wizard while I still had emotional energy to take on anything new. I'd have visited our members in nursing homes one more time.

Jesus predicted his own death plenty of times. His disciples never understood what he was talking about. Then when it happened, it all went quickly. Within a week, the world was upside down. He also predicted his resurrection, but they understood that even less.

Jesus knew. Change was coming. And change was not the end of the world, but the beginning of it. When Peter tried to tell Jesus his predictions were wrong, Jesus said, "Get behind me, Satan." (Mark 8:33)

I've always focused on the "Satan" part, but tonight I love the "behind me" part.

Jesus goes first. I may take some time to catch up.

Sleep well world. God holds you.

March 31, 2020
Day 17

Our kids, ages three and four, have gotten really good at washing their hands. They look like little doctors, lathering front, back, between the fingers, thumbs and wrists. They sing "Jesus Loves Me" to time their rinse.

I feel hemmed in by anxiety tonight. All these predictions. All this uncertainty. I can keep us fairly safe, but there are still too many unknowns. With kids in the mix, I've had moments of searing terror. *What if I can't protect them?*

I think I've swallowed some bad theology that says anxiety is sin because it means you don't trust God. Consider the lilies and all that.

I trust God. But I also recall that Jesus didn't throw himself off cliffs to prove God would save him.

Prayer and sleep help with the anxiety. So do information, exercise, and talking. But you know what else helps? Hearing "Jesus Loves Me" belted from the bathroom sink and knowing that we really are doing all we can.

Sleep well world. God holds you.

April 1, 2020
Day 18

We had our final Lent vespers service tonight. Five people in the sanctuary were joined by thirty-two others on Facebook. I read a favorite Bible passage: "We carry this precious message around in the unadorned clay pots of our ordinary lives." (2 Cor 4:7, MSG)

As I walked to my office afterward, I tripped over a large box.

The palms came.

We ordered them months ago. Normally we use them in worship on Palm Sunday, which is in five days.

Here's what's remarkable: I didn't spend an ounce of energy lamenting that we're not waving them en masse this year. Instead, I matter-of-factly stuck them in our empty office fridge and thought, *hmmm, I wonder how we'll use these?*

I have only a faint idea of how Holy Week is going to go. I've done precious little advance planning. Easter is ten days away. Normally I'd be freaking out, but now it seems almost laughable to think so far in advance.

And still, I'm positive these services are going to be meaningful—if also clumsy and unpolished. Maybe they'll be meaningful *because* they're clumsy and unpolished. Our humanity will be on full display. God's divinity will shine through.

The Bible passage continues: "We're not sure what to do, but we're sure God knows what to do." (2 Cor 4:8, MSG)

That sounds like very good news to me. I'll keep you posted on those palms.

Sleep well world. God holds you.

April 2, 2020
Day 19

Our almost five-year old daughter has learned to "read" a book. The only word in it is "hug." It's about a bereft little gorilla who wanders through the jungle crying "hug," until his mommy finds him and hugs him.[5]

This afternoon, our very clingy three-year old would not let me put her down. It was adorable, but also frustrating. It's hard to chop carrots with one hand. I was getting fed up when a neighbor who lives alone stopped by. She stayed outside and kept her distance. I remembered my abundance. I wish I could share these hugs.

The very existence of Jesus shows that God understands that bodies help us know that we are loved. I'm genuinely concerned for those with no physical contact. I have been suggesting that people get cats.

People who are isolated can't be hugged. They can't be in the physical presence of the church, "the body of Christ."

I notice people talking about flowers and food and the comfort of a warm blanket in almost sacramental tones. I pray tonight for people who need a hug. May one of these other ways that God inhabits the world help you know that you are loved.

As one friend always signs her emails, feel my hug.

Sleep well world. God holds you.

April 3, 2020
Day 20

Today my husband did the weekly grocery shopping. When he returned with the food, I felt irrationally afraid.

At my worst, my fear comes out in anger. I want to scream at people who are still taking this cavalierly or shirking their responsibilities to keep us all safe. Instead, I yelled at my husband to take off his shoes before he came inside in case they had virus on them.

At my best, my fear comes out in empathy. It connects me with other people's vulnerabilities. It makes me open-hearted.

I think it's the case that "don't be afraid" is the sentiment said the most in the gospels. In my experience of gospel-based communities, "don't be afraid" is never just lip service. It's followed with some earnest version of "what do you need so that you won't be afraid?"

I am profoundly grateful for people stocking the shelves and paying my salary and tending the sick. They're making it so that I actually don't need to be afraid. I see God in them. I pledge my absolute best to do the same in return.

And I am grateful for a husband who doesn't judge my fear, but instead scrupulously washes the groceries and leaves his shoes outside.

Sleep well world. God holds you.

April 5, 2020
Day 22

Palm Sunday.

I told you I'd report on what we did with our palms. We displayed some in the sanctuary during worship as is typical.

But we also displayed them outside the church as visible signs of the day. We've never done that before.

At home, I put palms on our car windshield, picture window and mailbox. I went a little overboard. Our house looks like it got leafleted by palms.

I encouraged my parishioners to do the same. Those who didn't have palms made their own using branches, leaves, or coloring pages, and posted them on front doors and windows. Some members delivered palms to the porches of people living in isolation.

The symbols of church are more important than ever because we don't have the symbol of the building to keep us connected.

I think of the hymn "God is Here!" It says, "Here are symbols to remind us of our lifelong need of grace."[6]

I'm guessing the hymn-writer assumed "here" would be the sanctuary. But now that every home has become a sanctuary, "here" is everywhere.

We've been conducting worship from the church building with only worship leaders present. It's become clear that it's too risky even to have a skeleton crew in person anymore, so we're moving worship entirely online. Today I toted home paraments and candles. I'm creating a worship space in our home for Holy Week services. Tomorrow I'll do a memorial service using Zoom from the altar set up in our spare bedroom. I'll put some palms on the altar too.

Here are symbols. On our front door. In the basement sanctuary.

Right. Here.

Sleep well world. God holds you.

April 6, 2020
Day 23

Today, I presided over a memorial service for a church member, Ann. It would have been her 95th birthday. Her death was not related to the virus.

She could not have imagined her memorial would be via Zoom with people from all around the country logging on. But she probably could have imagined that the eulogies would be glowing and the grief would be sincere. In a most humble way, she knew that she was loved.

There's a scene in scripture where one of Jesus' friends, Mary, takes expensive, fragrant oil and anoints Jesus as if anointing him for death. (John 12:1–3)

She didn't wait for him to die. She loved Jesus while he was alive.

Since this virus, I've said "I love you" much more freely. I've heard it more often too. Maybe one silver lining is that, newly aware of the possibility of death, we're more apt to lavish one another with love while we can.

For our dinner table tonight, I clipped a few sprigs of fragrant lavender from the garden. I rubbed some on my wrists. I did it to honor Ann and to remember that God's love is extravagant.

Sleep well world. God holds you.

April 7, 2020
Day 24

The singer John Prine died today, at age seventy-three. My dear pal and mentor, Bob Holum, introduced me to his music fifteen years ago. John Prine is intertwined with memories of Bob and Binnie's home, guitar and mandolin duets, the people of my internship at Luther Place Memorial Church, and the fullness of my young, earnest life in Washington, D.C.

I keep thinking, *Thank God this virus isn't affecting many children.* That's a major source of security as I tuck my girls in at night.

But that reminds me of what my husband said when he drove our newborn home from the hospital going a measly eight miles an hour. He said, "I want everyone to drive extra safely because I have a baby. But doesn't everyone in each of these cars matter to someone? Shouldn't we drive safely all the time?"

Everyone who is dying matters to somebody. I shudder at the numbers of seventy- and eighty-year olds who make my life meaningful and beautiful. I admit, I am afraid for them. And I'm afraid for me, without them.

So let's all keep up the distancing, advocating for personal protective equipment, and supporting leaders who make decisions that save lives. Let's take this thing as seriously as if it were affecting children.

Thanks for your life, John Prine.

Sleep well world. God holds you.

April 8, 2020
Day 25

Tonight, Jewish people begin Passover with new ways of telling ancient stories and sharing a sacred meal. Tomorrow, Maundy Thursday, in a ritual that echoes Passover, many Christians will do the same.

The Passover refers to the time when the Lord came to kill all the Egyptian firstborn sons but "passed over" the Hebrews' homes. (Exod 12)

The story used to bother me. I chafe at the idea that God saves some people at the expense of others. I'm not criticizing Judaism here; Christianity has the same problem.

But there's a political aspect to this story that's worth focusing on. Pharaoh's hard-hearted regime would not listen to the pleas of suffering people. God was on the side of the oppressed. It took drastic action to get Pharaoh to loosen his grip and set the people free.

I believe wholeheartedly in the saving love of Jesus. I also believe in the mystery and expansiveness of God, who works in all sorts of religions and people.

On this Passover, my prayer is that the angel of death passes over every home, hovel, tent or street corner tonight. Marked or unmarked, Christian, Jew, Muslim, atheist, you name it. All are precious.

I also pray that God helps us find a way to loosen the grip of modern day pharaohs, so that we can all be free.

Sleep well world. God holds you.

April 9, 2020
Day 26

Maundy Thursday.

My husband Ridgeway and I love having people over for dinner. We've served feasts of grilled salmon, roasted veggies, and wine. We've also served frozen pizza, sliced apples, and generic lemonade—especially when the kids were tiny and money was tight. No matter the food. The company was the most important thing.

Tonight, Paul contributed his handcrafted wine (Zin Boldly). Christy made the bread. Our table was one of fifty or so Zooming together and sharing a meal. Through the marvel of technology, we ate with friends and family. We ate as church. Grandma and Papa. Oma and Grandpa. Heather. Rachel. Mabel. Cilicia and Lucas and Petra. Kathleen and Marcia and Ardell and Linda. Jim and Adela and Kris and Steve. And so many others.

Jesus was there too.

The meal was satisfying, but the company was the most important thing.

Sleep well world. God holds you.

April 10, 2020
Day 27

Good Friday.

I've been emotional all day. Good Friday always gets to me and this year, it felt even more significant.

Before we began our evening service, I wasn't sure how it would end. Normally, we finish in darkness and silence, with just one candle lit. But this was Zoom. I didn't know how the candlelight would convey on video. I definitely didn't know how we'd handle the silence. In an act of over-preparedness, I cued up Gregorian chants on my phone to play in case the silence didn't work.

When worship ended, the silence was pitch perfect. The candle gave ancient light, so different from the light of a screen. A calm came over me as I prayed, watched the flame flicker, and let the music and words from worship reverberate in my mind.

That calm is still with me. It is not sorrow. It is peace.

Sleep well world. God holds you.

April 13, 2020
Day 30

Easter Monday.

I didn't write last night. I had every intention to, but I fell asleep on the couch, then in a kid's bed. Finally I dragged myself to my own bed and conked out again.

I think I'll be tired for a while. I loved putting together all the services last week. Easter Sunday was glorious and God's spirit was palpable, at least from my basement altar. But it was also exhausting.

I woke up today with my brain buzzing with new ideas and unfinished business. Names of people to thank and other people to check in on. Easter Sunday is a beginning, not an end. There is work to do!

But I stopped myself. God didn't raise Jesus from the dead so that I'd get worn out 2,000 years later. I can't continue at this pace and thankfully, the leadership of my church understands.

Today I rested. I didn't check email or texts or even look at the news. I cracked a novel. Drank tea. Napped and went on a long walk. And it was glorious too.

Sleep well world. God holds you.

April 14, 2020
Day 31

Leadership.

The outbreak at Smithfield meat packing plant in South Dakota has hit a personal nerve. My grandpa spent his entire career at Morrells, which eventually became Smithfield. I know that place.

My grandpa was a humble man. Eighth grade education. Wanted to tinker and fish and go to church. Needed his paycheck. Worked hard. Didn't ask for much.

From what I can tell, the governor of South Dakota has little regard for people like him, the people who put food on our tables. The people she serves.

I have a lot of sympathy for leaders who haven't been sure how to make the right decision. Been there. Made mistakes. But I've run out of sympathy for leaders who are puffed up with pride and willfully put their people in harm's way.

I'm grateful for the leaders who help me find my way through this. I think of the Episcopal bishop Marian Budde who was one of the first to urge churches to shut down in-person events. My own bishop Leila Ortiz gave thoughtful recommendations while also saying, "I trust you." Pastor Traci Blackmon of the United Church of Christ always has an eye for how people in poverty will be affected. I follow them because they are wise, compassionate, and brave.

Jesus was anointed by the Holy Spirit. Leadership was not conferred on him by an election or a title. It was demonstrated by his care and compassion for people.

In his time, he had very few followers. Over time, his style of leadership became the one to emulate: humble, powered by love, not self-serving, willing to challenge those who led people astray.

I truly pray for people who rely on their leaders to keep them safe, including the workers at Smithfield. I pray for leaders at every level as we see our way through this. It is hard to lead. I pray for followers too, that we all can discern which voices to follow and which ones to ignore.

Sleep well world. God holds you.

April 15, 2020
Day 32

Our eldest daughter doesn't know the phrase "the day after tomorrow." Instead, she calls it "tomorrow tomorrow." Sometimes she'll string tomorrows together and ask about "tomorrow tomorrow tomorrow tomorrow," a.k.a. four days from now.

It seems like we're getting collectively itchy to know an end date. From "we'll reopen May 5th" to "we'll be social distancing until 2022," there's a wide range of predictions for when we'll be back to normal. How many tomorrows will it be?

I'm resisting the need to know. God gave the Israelites manna enough for the day, every day, as they wandered through the wilderness. That's where the idea of daily bread comes from. (Exod 16)

The word *manna* literally means "what is this?" The promise of daily bread is connected with the experience of bewilderment.

The inability to plan for the future is a kind of wilderness. Still, I know what tomorrow looks like. And what we will eat. And I trust God's promise that when tomorrow tomorrow comes, we'll have what we need for that day too.

Sleep well world. God holds you.

April 16, 2020
Day 33

A few years ago I traveled to Haiti because our church was helping build a health clinic. We visited a variety of medical facilities, from a well-funded hospital to a low-income infirmary. As I watched terribly impoverished people wait for hours to see doctors in ill-equipped rooms, the contrast became stark: health is tied to wealth.

Of course you don't need to travel to notice this. In the United States, it's well-documented that populations which have been systematically kept from creating wealth—including disproportional numbers of African-Americans—have higher infection and mortality rates from COVID-19.

I'm going to state the obvious: Wealthy people have better health care—and better health—than poor people.

There's no way that's OK with God.

Jesus was all about healing people, including those with no option but to beg. Jesus came to bring "good news to the poor." (Luke 4:18)

Our health care system does not work for poor people. I'm no expert on health care policy, and I know I'm saying nothing new here. But I think it's worth stating the obvious because it makes it obvious something is wrong.

Maybe this crisis will give us the impetus to change.

Sleep well world. God holds you.

April 18, 2020
Day 35

News.

Today I worked on a yard project that involves laying down newspaper and layering mulch on top. My *Washington Post* subscription is digital so a church member gave me newspapers. They were from last week. As I spread out the papers, I felt like I was seeing headlines from a different world.

Typically, I read the *Post* daily, and I listen to NPR whenever I'm in the car. I read two or three magazines a week too. I used to enjoy the news and I think that to be a responsible citizen and a relevant pastor, I need to know what's going on.

But for a month, I've only had energy for my bubble of home, church, family, friends, neighbors. I check headlines for five minutes and most days, that's all I can take.

I'm having a hard time not feeling guilty about all the ways I've stopped engaging with wider issues.

But I don't know what to do about it. I just can't muster the energy. I am overwhelmed. I'm trying to treat myself with grace.

A famous theologian once quipped that a pastor needs to have the Bible in one hand and the newspaper in the other.

I've got the Bible. Scripture has never been so alive for me.

But the paper? For now, it is under the mulch. At least it's doing some good there.

Sleep well world. God holds you.

April 19, 2020
Day 36

For the last two Sundays, our church has sung a version of Psalm 136 written by one of our musicians, Paul. The chorus says, "For his steadfast love endures forever."

Today, our four-year old told me it was her favorite song from worship. She doesn't understand all the words but that hasn't stopped her. She sang it all afternoon, belting out the words "love" and "forever," and thoughtfully trying to remember the words "steadfast" and "endures."

Some twenty miles from our house, a man wrote a melody. And some 3,000 years ago, a different man wrote a prayer. And while worshiping via Zoom from our living room couch, my little girl learned a song that might be in her heart forever.

This sickness has taken a lot, including our ability to be together in person. The distance is real. But we are still a community gathered for worship.

"Give thanks to the Lord, for he is good. For his steadfast love endures forever."[7]

Sleep well world. God holds you.

April 20, 2020
Day 37

In staff Bible study today we read Acts 2. Peter, a disciple of Jesus, preached to a crowd about Jesus' resurrection and death, saying, "You crucified him." That "you" signified not only the particular individuals who executed Jesus, but all those who let it happen. It included those who benefitted from the injustices Jesus' life exposed. It included Peter himself.

The listeners were "cut to the heart." They asked themselves, "What should we do?" Peter told them, "Repent and be baptized." In other words, "Be forgiven, change, and join us." Three thousand people were baptized. By the end of the chapter, they held all things in common.

As I witness the stories of COVID-19 deaths and devastations, I am "cut to the heart" by an all-too-familiar pattern. Those most harmed are people in poverty, people in prison, people without legal status, people of color, and people on the margins. It's not surprising that there's significant overlap between white supremacist groups and the protestors demanding that society reopen too soon.

Who is being crucified? What can we do?

Some of the best stuff in the gospel is captured in the word "repent." Peter knows firsthand that forgiveness is liberating. Change is possible. A new community can be formed.

God help us. God help me. Let the Holy Spirit come. Let this moment be for repentance and for the common good.

Sleep well world. God holds you.

April 21, 2020
Day 38

Our congregation has just received guidance on how to count worshipers for online services. By some measures, we've quintupled our reach. I'm excited about that. I want to share the good news.

At the same time, I am wary of equating success with large numbers. Some tiny churches are beacons of God's grace. Some mega-churches are corrupt. I've never been able to nail down the relationship between fidelity to the gospel and church growth.

On the eve of Earth Day, I'm reminded of Dr. Seuss's ecotale *The Lorax*. He teaches that growing bigger for biggering's sake can have disastrous consequences.[8]

Jesus met one woman at the empty tomb. Maybe it was three. Two more people on the road to Emmaus. Yes, the news spread, but it started small.

In a different time, I would focus more on how to capitalize on the growth of online worship. In this time, I can't. I still only have energy to think small as I try to turn my uncertainty and outrage into peaceable productivity.

Kids. Seeds. Individual relationships. The church I serve. I hope that if in these small things I am faithful to the gospel, God will take care of the growth.

Sleep well world. God holds you.

April 22, 2020
Day 39

Earth Day.

I've never been a climate change denier. In high school in the late 1980s, I wrote a paper about the destruction of rainforests and the greenhouse effect. Even then, the science was clear and terrifying.

Until coronavirus, climate change was my main experience of existential despair. I don't use the word *despair* lightly. I've had wake-up-in-the-middle-of-the-night panic about the warming Earth. It's made me wrestle with God and come to the edge of faith.

Like I said, I've never been a climate change denier. But I have been a "people can change for the good" denier. And I've been a "God can turn this ship around" denier.

The coronavirus is undeniably awful. Yet our response contains hope. Systems can change quickly when people realize our lives are at stake, and our love can make a difference. It's given me faith that the kind of change needed to reverse our ecological trajectory is possible.

It's also made my trust in God more alive than ever. My despair has been met with renewed faith. God's power is palpable and unleashed.

I have ridiculous amounts of hope for the future. Happy Earth Day.

Sleep well world. God holds you.

April 23, 2020
Day 40

Day forty. The quarantine is over, right?

The word quarantine comes from the word forty. It is the number of days ships had to stay in port during the black plague. Forty is also the number of years the Israelites wandered in the wilderness. It's the number of days Noah's ark floated and Jesus fasted.

Forty is a Biblical number that marks the end of a trial period, but we're not done.

When I started writing this on March 15th, the first Sunday our church went virtual, I thought it would last a few weeks. We're on day forty and it appears we are going to be in quarantine for a long time, even if the most stringent restrictions lift soon.

We're on a journey, not in a port.

Scripture is full of roads and pathways, people setting off toward the unknown and meeting God along the way. One of my favorite Bible stories is the Road to Emmaus. Grieving disciples met the resurrected Jesus on the road, not in safe harbor.

What was true forty days ago is true now and will be true every day that lies ahead. God joins us on the way and gives us strength to keep going.

Sleep well world. God holds you.

P.S. At the beginning, I planned to write every night except one sabbath a week. I need two nights off. So I will take Fridays and Saturdays off and write again on Sunday.

April 26, 2020
Day 43

On Friday, a woman in my congregation died from COVID-19. It's our first such death.

She was ninety years old and had underlying health conditions, so her death isn't exactly a tragedy. But without this virus, she would be alive, her husband of sixty-seven years would not be so disoriented, and her death would not have been as lonely.

Today I feel the longing to move past this quickly. I want the coronavirus to disappear. I miss my friends. I'm no longer enchanted with online worship. Heck, I want to renovate my kitchen! It was finally underway after seven years of dreaming and then. Stopped.

It's that grief again. Wanting things to be different. Aware of all that's been lost.

I preached today about the importance of grief. I was preaching to myself because I don't want to grieve. I'd much rather be chipper and cheerful.

I have no choice. I am sad. I'm going to carve out time in my schedule to grieve. I will be still. Alone. Maybe go for a walk. Maybe take a nap. I worry that if I don't, I will get blindsided by grief in the guise of anger or resentment or burn out. Maybe that will still happen. All I can do is try to cry my tears and take my time.

Grief is hard, but it's not the worst thing. It's how we get through. We will get through.

Sleep well world. God holds you.

April 27, 2020
Day 44

Thanks to everyone who has reached out in sympathy for the death I wrote about yesterday. It is wonderful to be cared for.

Today I was itching to move my body. I hauled my old bike from the back of the garage and pumped up the tires. I wobbled around the backyard to test the brakes, then did a couple of loops through the neighborhood. Fifteen minutes. Just enough to remember how much I love riding a bike.

Zooming down a hill I laughed as I remembered the original meaning of the word *zoom*. As my legs struggled to crest that same hill a few minutes later, I felt like a person, not just a face behind a screen. I felt playful, childlike and strong. I felt free. I felt like myself.

During this quarantine, parts of my identity have been on overdrive (caregiver, housekeeper, Facebook maven), but other parts have almost disappeared (reader, athlete, host of dinner parties).

I miss myself. I miss the balance of all my parts. I was grateful today for fifteen minutes on a bike and the wholeness that came with it.

Sleep well world. God holds you.

April 28, 2020
Day 45

What do we have in common? Typically I'd answer that question with personal characteristics. Are you from Minnesota? A mother of preschoolers? A fan of the band U2? If you say yes, I'm bound to feel some kinship.

In the Biblical book of Acts, the early church is described as having "all things in common." (Acts 2:44) The writer of Acts isn't talking about characteristics, he's talking about resources. They shared it all.

Their impulse to hold all things in common was a sign that they trusted God.

When I'm secure, I'm also generous. When I'm afraid, I get stingy, storing up treasure for myself and trying to go it alone.

This virus has revealed just how much we share. It's also shown how dangerous the fiction of independence can be.

What do we have in common? The power grid. Food production. The well-being of our children. Our planet. Our future.

What do we have in common? Everything. Most especially a loving God who we can trust to provide all we need, emphasis on the "we."

Sleep well world. God holds you.

April 29, 2020
Day 46

"The Lord will keep your going out and your coming in." (Ps 121:8)

We went out tonight. It has been a draining few days and I needed a boost. I craved a drive and some comfort food. Our plans weren't big—drive to a burger joint and get take-out—but it was enough to give us some excitement.

It was the first time the kids have been in a car for forty-six days. They were giddy. They shouted at each landmark and shrieked with delight when we passed their daycare.

I was giddy too. It felt so good to be out together, wind in our hair, songs from *Frozen 2* on the radio.

By the time we got to the drive-thru, the thrill was fading. We were masked, gloved and sanitized, but still I felt anxious. I also felt ashamed. Did we just do something stupid, putting ourselves and others at risk? Rather than stick with our original plan to eat in the parking lot, I just wanted to get home.

On the way back, we passed the hospital where our girls were born. They eagerly pointed it out, as they always do, but something was amiss.

The block was filled with police cars and firetrucks. Groups of people in masks were lined up out front. We don't know what was going on, but it seemed ominous. I was suddenly nervous and sad, reminded that things are not all right.

Home again, we ate our food in safe isolation on blankets in the front yard, volleying conversations with neighbors across the street and playing tag until the sun went down.

The Lord watches over the going out, yes.

And also, the coming in.

Sleep well world. God holds you.

P.S. I learned after I posted this that the activity at the hospital was actually a parade to boost hospital workers' spirits. It's worthy of reflection that I saw a parade and thought it was a protest. Clearly I am on edge.

April 30, 2020
Day 47

Today was the memorial service for the woman who died last week. Usually for a memorial service, floral arrangements that sometimes cost hundreds of dollars are delivered to the church.

For today's service, church friends dropped off a bouquet of colorful tulips and branches of pink azaleas clipped from their yard.

The flowers were beautiful, meaningful, and free. It was one of hundreds of times this COVID life has made me think, why don't we always do it this way?

There's a flip side of course. An entire industry has been built on arranging and delivering flowers. People will experience financial insecurity if we no longer need fancy bouquets.

From oil producers to restaurateurs to florists to—yes—pastors, COVID-related changes bring terrifying financial insecurity. But they also bring the possibility of a new economy driven by values like compassion, simplicity, neighborliness, and a livable planet.

I don't want fear to keep me from stepping into this new world. Instead, I want to look at the lilies of the field and trust that God will provide.

After all, the azaleas are fading, but the roses are just about to bloom.

Sleep well world. God holds you.

May 3, 2020
Day 50

My soul was restored this weekend. A canoe trip. Fresh radishes. A weekend off from preaching. A socially-distanced visit with my cousins. I even got a nap.

There was a time in the not-so-distant past that I would have felt bad about enjoying a day like this while the death toll, unemployment, and bad behavior are all on the rise.

But God keeps showing me that joy and peace are gifts to be cherished, especially when the world is in so much turmoil.

Revival is God's work. We aren't only made for labor and mourning, for the burden of healing and the relentlessness of peace-making.

We are also made for rest and laughter, for being healed and at peace.

Sleep well world. God holds you.

May 4, 2020
Day 51

One of the assigned scriptures for Sunday is the story of Stephen the martyr in Acts 6–7.

Stephen led the feeding ministry of the earliest church. He made sure widows could eat.

For such a crime, he was brought to trial. The accusation? Changing customs and following Jesus.

In his defense, he pointed out the long history of nations killing prophets and propping up unjust leaders. He was stoned to death by a crowd that was outraged by his truth-telling.

I see obvious connections with the protests of the past weeks. A violent crowd, armed for blood. Willful ignorance of history. Treating those who serve others as if they are the problem.

Contrast that outrage with Stephen, a witness that upset the status quo because of who he served: hungry widows, the crucified Jesus.

Stephen didn't fight back with violence. He was full of grace. His dying words contain a key that unlocks a different future: "Lord, do not hold this sin against them." (Acts 7:60)

Sleep well world. God holds you.

May 5, 2020
Day 52

In the first weeks of the pandemic, I was in triage mode. My priorities were dictated by immediate concerns: *How does Zoom talk to Facebook? Who is watching our children? Is everyone in the congregation OK? How much longer can we go without milk?*

Now, as the country is opening up, my energy and mental space are opening up too. The problem? I can't figure out my priorities.

I can easily recall how I used to spend my time, how I structured a day. Some of my habits were beneficial. But some were not. The same is true for the church and society.

I sense that it's more important than ever to open up slowly, and not just to keep people healthy. I fear if we go quickly, we will default to a past that didn't always serve.

I think of the sisters Mary and Martha. Jesus critiqued Martha for being so distracted that she missed an important moment. Jesus praised Mary for her focus on "only one thing." (Luke 10:38–42)

My prayer tonight is for focus and discernment. I pray that I don't jam up the future with the priorities of the past but instead let God show me the better way.

Sleep well world. God holds you.

May 6, 2020
Day 53

For the bedtime story tonight, we pulled out our gorgeous children's book of Noah's Ark.[9] It's all pictures, no words. I love "reading" with our kids as they tell the story, but I fear the day they narrate the page where the flood begins.

On that page, there's a succession of paintings of the poor elephants who were left off the ark. As the water rises, they're up to their knees, then up to their heads. Finally, they disappear.

With great harm, too much of Christianity has echoed this interpretation of Noah's ark: God saves some people; the rest are sunk.

I don't buy it. I cannot believe in the narrowness of God's salvation. Thankfully, there's plenty of scriptural and theological basis to draw a different conclusion. God loves the whole world. That's the point of Jesus.

Right now, my family and church are mostly safe and sound. It could be easy to shut the doors of the ark and count my blessings.

Because of Jesus, I don't want to. Because of Jesus, I refuse to accept the proposition that only some people can be saved. And I don't just mean spiritually saved. I mean healed and fed and housed and financially solvent and able to live a pleasant life.

I'm grateful for images that disturb me. For the picture of the elephants drowning. For stories of food lines and data about financial duress. I'm thankful for journalists who keep exposing how people with black and brown skin bear the brunt of society's sin.

For prophets who disturb my peace. They help me see what's wrong, so that I can ask God to help us make it right.

I want to rewrite the Noah story. I think God can save those poor elephants. I believe there's room for everybody in the ark.

Sleep well world. God holds you.

May 7, 2020
Day 54

I'm supersaturated tonight. Too much work. Too much Zoom. And too much news, much of it falling smack in the middle of a demoralizing Venn diagram:

A: Things I care about.
B: Things that are awful.
C: Things I can't control.

I think what's got me down tonight is feeling powerless. It's bigger than the coronavirus, though that's in there of course. It's also the gutting of our nation's best institutions, the pervasive racism in our legal system, the chaos of the news-reporting industry itself, and feeling like there's nothing I can do about any of it.

In the gospel for Sunday, Jesus tells his disciples, "Whatever you ask for in my name, I will do it." (John 14:14) What a display of power! What an offer! At first glance it seems arrogant, unrealistic, and dangerous. After all, how many faithful people have begged to God only to have their prayers go unanswered and their faith destroyed?

It's important to know that when Jesus made the offer, he was echoing what an evil leader, Herod, said earlier to his step-daughter in a show of power meant to flatter dinner guests: "Whatever you ask me, I will give you." (Mark 6:23) She asked for the head of John the Baptist on a platter. Her wish was granted.

People eager to prove their power can quickly turn dangerous, even lethal.

That's not what Jesus is about. Jesus doesn't just give us what we want. He has nothing to prove. He gives what we ask for "in his name." In the name of the one who was about to be crucified.

Jesus doesn't mean we can become all-powerful. Instead, he shows us that we can access the power Jesus had on the cross, power to be intimately connected to God, even when the world has taken everything.

God always gives some power. Power to pray. Power to tell the truth. Power to forgive. Power to dream. Power to hope, in Jesus' name.

Sleep well world. God holds you.

May 10, 2020
Day 57

Mother's Day.

One of the hardest parts of COVID-life is not knowing when I'll see my parents again. I live in Virginia. They live in Minnesota. We're hoping there will be reliable testing so we can go there safely in late summer. Of course, we won't know that until late summer. I'm not holding my breath. Realistically, there's a good chance I won't see them for a year.

In a fit of sentimentality, I have made our daughters promise that we'll all live next door to one another when they're adults. If I am truly my mother's daughter, I won't hold them to that promise.

My mother never held my decisions hostage to her needs. It's one of the most enduring gifts she gave me. That meant dropping me off at airports not knowing when she'd see me again, driving me across-country for a move, and letting me go.

Coronavirus has shown me that physical distance really does matter. Even with Zoom and FaceTime, something is lost by living far from the ones I love.

I'm not gonna lie, I'll be thrilled if I can live near our daughters when they are adults. But I'll be more thrilled if they can say about me what I can say about my mom: She is content in her life and eager to help me find contentment in mine, even if it is different from hers. She just wants me to be happy.

I love you Mom.

Sleep well world. God holds you.

May 11, 2020
Day 58

"I will not leave you orphaned." (John 14:18)

In Jesus' farewell to his followers, he promised that the Spirit of God would be with them even after he was gone. It always sounds to me like a commencement speech—part nostalgia, part pep talk. It's a divine "you got this," and by "you," Jesus means "you plus God."

I've been outraged and terrified by the leadership of our country. By contrast, I've been impressed with how many people, seeing the vacuum of leadership at the top, have bypassed traditional channels of power.

A faith-based organization in Baltimore bought tents for homeless people because shelters were unsafe. A nearby church partnered with chef José Andrés to become a World Central Kitchen site. Our congregation is poised to expand a staff position for community outreach.

Yes, I wish our government were different. That's an understatement. And yes, I do think people of faith need to keep up the hard press of advocating for compassionate policies from our elected leaders. Still, it gives me hope to remember that the government doesn't hold all the power, not by a long shot.

Jesus may have said goodbye, but we have not been orphaned. God's Spirit is here. We got this.

Sleep well world. God holds you.

May 12, 2020
Day 59

Bleak day. Another congregant died from the virus. Employees at the grocery store where we shop have tested positive. NPR aired a story featuring a nearby neighborhood that's one of our state's hot spots.

There's a theme here: extreme vulnerability. The congregant was in a memory care facility and completely dependent on his poorly paid care-givers. The grocery store employees need their minimum wage jobs to survive. The nearby neighborhood is impoverished, crowded, and full of people who have to work without safety nets.

A good society should care for its most vulnerable. Instead, we're throwing them under the bus. Our leaders keep feeding us a line that this is inevitable, saying that we have to choose between people's lives and society's economic well-being.

When Jesus told Judas, "You will always have the poor with you," (Mark 14:7) he wasn't talking about the inevitability of poverty. He was talking about Judas' lack of moral imagination. Judas was both holding the common purse and, not surprisingly, stealing from it.

It's not that hard to imagine a world where we don't have to choose between saving people from poverty and saving people's lives. I don't know the mechanism for how we can do it, but I can imagine it. I know I'm not alone.

Sleep well world. God holds you.

May 13, 2020
Day 60

Today our oldest daughter turned five. We couldn't throw a traditional party, so we were worried it would be a bummer of a birthday. To compensate, we planned a day full of little surprises, bought a few too many presents, and painted an old bedsheet with "Maggie is 5!" to hang in our front yard so everyone would know.

We need not have worried. People came out for our girl.

A neighbor snuck over at night and chalked a birthday greeting in our driveway. Another neighbor delivered balloons. Church members did a drive-by hello. Friends sent videos of themselves singing "Happy Birthday." Both sides of the family hopped in on Zoom calls. Even the UPS guy got in on the action, leaving a congratulatory note on the door. And the highlight? Neighbors lined the sidewalk and cheered for our makeshift birthday parade.

It's like everyone knew it might be sad to turn five in the middle of a pandemic, so they did what they could do to make it great. There was no one huge thing, just loads of little ways people showed their love. It added up to the best birthday a five-year old could ask for. I'm a grateful, tired momma.

Sleep well world. God holds you.

May 14, 2020
Day 61

"If suffering is God's will, it is better to suffer because you did good than because you did evil." (1 Pet 3:17)

I don't like to suffer. I like a firm mattress, a well-stocked fridge, and a society that's built to cater to my needs. I can easily convince myself that's what God wants for me too. An easy life. The absence of pain.

I have a hard time with this stuff from 1 Peter. I want to look past the phrase "suffering is God's will" not just because I like creature comforts, but because I cling to the phrase "God is love," (1 John 4:8) and those two phrases seem incompatible.

At the same time, the existence of suffering is obvious and I respect a worldview that puts God at the center and relates everything—even suffering—to God. It's the worldview I strive for. I want God to shape me, not the other way around. So I look again.

In studying 1 Peter, I notice it indicates that not all suffering is equal. Some suffering leads to more suffering, but some suffering leads to good. And that, too, is obvious, as countless nurses and bus drivers and grocery store employees have shown in recent weeks.

I think we call that kind of suffering *sacrifice*—literally "drawing closer to the sacred." I think we call it love. Maybe the point is that we don't get to choose *if* we will suffer. What we get to choose is if we bear our suffering with resentment or with love. Lord, help us choose well.

Sleep well world. God holds you.

May 17, 2020
Day 64

Like many churches, Peace's Zoom didn't work this morning. Our team scrambled and responded swiftly, but couldn't solve it. We were stymied. When I finally discovered it was a problem with Zoom worldwide, I was relieved. At least it wasn't my ineptitude that kept people from worshiping.

It also wasn't anyone else's, not really, not even Zoom's (though I may have let a curse word slip their direction). Three months ago, the Zoom company didn't know they'd be the primary way the whole world would connect. They had no idea they'd need to scale up quite so dramatically. There are bound to be hiccups.

It's so easy to judge using old standards.

Today, I remembered how new this still is and how much we're asking of one another. It makes me want to lower my expectations and increase my gratitude.

I also remembered that the good people of our church will come through for one another in predictably kindhearted ways, no matter the technology. Even had it been my fault, I would have been forgiven. Our church is a church of grace.

We recovered. It was stressful, but hardly the end of the world. We worshiped. Our community stuck in there for one another. God was near.

Sleep well world. God holds you.

May 18, 2020
Day 65

I once got to hear Sam Nzima give a talk. He's a South African photographer who took an iconic photo of a child, Hector Pieterson, who was shot and killed during the Soweto protests in 1976. That picture went around the world and changed the global response to apartheid.

Nzima said something that stuck with me: "If it's not recorded, it didn't happen."[10] He wasn't commenting on the actuality of an event, but pointing out that without journalists reporting the truth, people in power can too easily manipulate reality.

I thought of Nzima because on Sunday, our church service was photographed by journalists who work for a news outlet which is documenting faith communities' response to the pandemic. One photographer took photos of me presiding from my basement sanctuary while another was at a member's home, photographing their family at worship on their laptop.

After looking at our pictures (they're really cool), I started scrolling through the news outlet's website. I was captivated by all the photos these folks have taken in the last two months.

It got me thinking about all the moments that journalists document, creating a body of work dedicated to truth. Much of it is as unglamorous as hanging out in a pastor's cramped basement on a Sunday morning. Still, it all adds up, and sometimes they get the picture that can change the world.

During the trial that would end in his execution as an enemy of the state, Jesus told Pilate, "I have come to bear witness to the truth." Pilate responded, "What is truth?" (John 18:38)

Praying tonight for the safety and courage of journalists who bear witness to the truth. May their holy work bend our world toward justice.

Sleep well world. God holds you.

May 19, 2020
Day 66

Prayer.

I wish I could say I've prayed more than ever since this all began. The truth is that prayer takes time and sustained attention, things that have been in short supply.

I spent a lot of time in prayer today. I prayed for specific people in my congregation. You may be asking, "What does a pastor do when she says 'I prayed for people today.'?" Here's what I do:

I make a list. It's as if each person on my list is a statue on a big table. In my mind, I pick one up, hold it to the light and examine it. I turn it over. I look closely.

Focused on the person, I imagine all the different parts of their life and try to connect them to God. It's like I'm pulling them close and asking God to come close too. I bring to mind their family, their work, their health, their spiritual life, their struggles, their friendships, their rough edges, their talents and their joys. I think about the things I know and the things I don't know. This takes a few minutes. Then I thank God for them and ask for God to be with them in a way they can sense today. I gently put them down, and go to the next person on my list.

That's what I do. It was good to get back to it today.

Sleep well world. God holds you.

May 20, 2020
Day 67

Water.

Parts of Bangladesh and Michigan are under water. A lot of indebted people are too. Disasters are even more catastrophic when poured on top of a pandemic.

The psalmist wrote about the rising noise of the sea. The deafening sound makes it impossible to hear anything but its thunderous power. (Ps 93)

In the Bible, water can be a metaphor for chaos. We are swimming in it.

Water can also be a means of salvation. Prescribed floods and parted seas and wells that never run dry. Little boats seek out survivors and homes are opened to those in need. Climate scientists warn to prepare for the floods to come, so that we may be saved.

We start worship each Sunday with a remembrance of baptism. From their homes, worshipers dip their fingers in bowls of water and trace a cross on their foreheads. Because I am alone in the room, I mark myself. Even so, the water always surprises me. It is fresh and cool.

There is God's majesty, dripping down my arm. Rising above the chaos. Cutting through the noise. Bringing holy order to a raging world.

Sleep well world. God holds you.

May 21, 2020

Day 68

Memorial Day Weekend.

Sibs and Spice. That's me and my four siblings, plus our spouses. (Aptly, they named themselves the Spice). They're all cool, interesting, kind people. Good company. We love being together.

The last time we were all in the same place was six months ago, Thanksgiving in Minnesota. Somewhere between the cranberry sauce and the pumpkin pie, we realized that in the spring, my oldest brother and my husband would both turn fifty. Certainly, a celebration was in order.

We decided to take a weekend away. We've never done anything like that, but with kids getting older and jobs stabilizing, it seemed possible. After bouncing ideas around, we made a plan.

Nashville. No kids. Music, food, cocktails, dancing, lounging, cards, laughter, more music.

You guessed it: we planned it for Memorial Day weekend.

We all arranged childcare (no small feat with sixteen kids involved!), got off work, found flights, rented an Airbnb for ten, and googled music venues.

You know the rest of the story. None of us will be boarding a plane tomorrow.

All day, I've been thinking, *In the alternate universe, I'd be packing, prepping the kids for our departure, and making a list for the babysitter.*

All day I've been thinking, *I'd see some of my favorite people in the whole world, tomorrow.*

I know this isn't life or death. In the grand scheme, it's no big deal. The weekend at home will be fine. The family will rally. Maybe we'll do a Zoom with the Minnesota crew. The Sibs and Spice will make the trip happen another year. But dang. I'm really bummed out tonight.

If anyone needs me tomorrow, I'll be nursing my disappointment, requesting songs from my guitar-playing husband, texting with the Sibs and Spice, and dreaming of a different universe.

Sleep well world. God holds you.

May 24, 2020
Day 71

At one point this afternoon, my husband was prepping a canvas for a painting, I was setting up my pottery wheel, and both girls were doing their own messy art projects. This happened quite naturally and without coordination, but there was a reason for it.

We'd all been inspired in church.

For the past three weeks, our church has included a "Creative Offering" in our liturgy. Today, artist Marni shared paintings she has made during the pandemic. She connected the experience of painting them with her faith. They were breathtaking, whimsical, and powerful. God was evident.

Afterward she led a simple line drawing exercise called "Signs of the Spirit." She primed our creative juices. We'll use the artwork next week on Pentecost Sunday.

With everything going on in the world, taking time to do art together might seem like it should be low on the priority list. But I think it's one of the most important things churches can do. A community that creates together is alive with God's spirit.

Everyone is in the process of creating new ways of being. I find it thrilling but also exhausting. Sometimes I don't want to have to face another challenge or come up with some alternative way to do church.

Today I tapped into a different kind of creativity: the kind that's pure play. It comes when I'm coloring with the kids or making pottery or gardening. It fills me back up.

Who knows if any of the projects my family started will get finished. That's not the point. For a short while today, we each got lost in the pleasure of creativity without consequence or purpose. It was good.

Sleep well world. God holds you.

SECTION 2

LOOKING IN ON PENTECOST:
THE WORLD'S ON FIRE
May 26, 2020 – August 2, 2020

"When the day of Pentecost had come, they were all together in one place. And suddenly from heaven there came a sound like the rush of a violent wind, and it filled the entire house where they were sitting. Divided tongues, as of fire, appeared among them, and a tongue rested on each of them. All of them were filled with the Holy Spirit." (Acts 2:1–4)

~~~

"I can't breathe."
—*George Floyd, May 25, 2020* [1]

"When historians pick up their pens to write the story of the 21st century, let them say that it was your generation who laid down the heavy burdens of hate at last and that peace finally triumphed over violence, aggression and war. So I say to you, walk with the wind, brothers and sisters, and let the spirit of peace and the power of everlasting love be your guide."
—*Representative John Lewis, farewell essay published the day of his funeral, July 30, 2020* [2]

May 26, 2020
Day 73

The news of the day from my hometown is horrific. In Minneapolis, a black man was brutally killed by a white cop. He committed no crime that warranted such a response.

This pattern is entrenched and it is evil. It existed long before coronavirus, but it sure seems that coronavirus has helped fan racist flames.

White supremacy is kin to many of the "you can't make me wear a mask" sentiments. COVID-19 has disproportionately affected African American and Latino communities. It makes it too easy for white leaders to trivialize the damage. Plus, with all the generalized fear and anxiety, people are looking for someone to blame and someone to shame.

At one point, it seemed like coronavirus was bringing out our best "we're in this together" instincts. Now, it seems to be ripping us farther apart. I fear we're living in a tinderbox.

Enter the Pentecost. Flames are a dominant metaphor for the Holy Spirit. Fire is refining and powerful. It can destroy, but it also can be for good. It gave the disciples power to speak new languages and build bridges toward people they'd been isolated from before.

We are promised the Holy Spirit's power and fire. If we're in a tinderbox, may it be one in which people burst into surprising acts of courage, unity, justice and love. Come, Holy Spirit, come.

Sleep well world. God holds you.

P.S. If anyone's keeping track, you'll notice I didn't write yesterday. I had a lovely Memorial Day holiday chilling with my family and just couldn't muster the energy for thought. This is going on much longer than I'd thought. But I'll keep writing.

May 27, 2020
Day 74

The Psalm assigned for Sunday is Psalm 104. It's a song of the harmony and diversity of creation. Birds nest in treetops and the creature Leviathan plays in the depths of the sea. God is both powerful and benevolent, responsible for feeding the creatures and ensuring that all will be satisfied. The assigned section is verses 24-34 and 35b. That means that one half of one verse, 35a, was omitted.

You might be asking, "What is 35a?"

"Let sinners be consumed from the earth, and let the wicked be no more." (Ps 104:35a)

Hmm.

That line isn't included in the reading for Sunday presumably because it is jarring and hard to hear. Jesus said, "Love your enemies." (Matt 5:44) That's a far cry from "let sinners be consumed."

I get it. A theology of grace leads us toward a God who forgives sins and away from a God who smites the wicked. Plus, any student of the Lutheran Confessions knows that there's no such thing as a sinner who can just be plucked up and removed from the otherwise perfect world. We're all sinners in need of redeeming.

Even so, I would include 35a.

One of the great things about the Psalms is their honesty. This line acknowledges a truth we know all too well: in the goodness of God's creation, wickedness wreaks havoc.

It's a lament about the world as it is. It's also a confession. I can't pray it without realizing that I'm asking for the wickedness that lives within me to be removed, something only God can do.

This line echoes the honest, disturbing prayers in my heart lately, prayers that include an end to the power of people who have become consumed in wickedness and sin.

I don't want to sanitize my prayers right now. It's not like God just does all my bidding anyway. I think God wants to hear that we know some things are terribly wrong. And we need help.

These hard lines only add to the point of the Psalm. Nothing is more powerful than God's creative goodness. Praise the Lord.

Sleep well world. God holds you.

May 28, 2020
Day 75

One theme of pandemic life is how much I toggle between sorrow and joy.

One hundred thousand COVID deaths in the United States. Dangerously politicized public health decisions. Minneapolis boiling over with the toxic brew of racism. I shed tears of sadness today.

Kindergarten orientation. Surprise gifts left on the front stoop. The holy wedding of two people who met just weeks before the pandemic began. I also cried tears of joy.

The marriage prayers included this petition:

> Most gracious God, you have made us in your image and given us over to one another's care. Hear the prayers of your people, that unity may overcome division, hope vanquish despair, and joy conquer sorrow.[3]

It's a prayer that applies far beyond a wedding. It's a prayer for tonight.

Sleep well world. God holds you.

May 31, 2020
Day 78

When I started these faith-based reflections, I had no idea to what extent we'd need reminders of God's presence. I also didn't predict that coronatime would intersect so profoundly with the movement for racial justice.

Today is Pentecost, when the Holy Spirit came to a group of Jesus' followers as they huddled together in an upper room. The Holy Spirit came as noise, wind, fire, speech.

Outside the house, their co-religionists heard the clamor and were drawn to it. Some thought those spirited folks were drunk and they shamed them, trying to dismiss their power. Others thought they were speaking God's truth and were soon converted. (Acts 2)

I have always heard this story as if I were represented by those in the upper room. I'm a baptized, Holy Spirit-inspired disciple of Jesus. A card-carrying member of his church on a mission. There have been times in my life when that was the right parallel to draw.

Today, it is clear to me that I am on the outside. Some other community—many of them my co-religionists—is fueled by the Holy Spirit. They are speaking in sounds and symbols that are unfamiliar, yet in which I hear God's truth.

I am drawn to them, even as my peace is disturbed by them. They are inviting me into a deeper peace. Peace with justice. Peace for all. I want to be converted, and not just in name. I want to be part of ushering in a new era that is reason for praise. Shalom.

I pray that God keeps drawing me closer to that which is holy, even if it is also unfamiliar, chaotic, and scary.

The Spirit is moving. She is moving indeed.

Sleep well world. God holds you.

June 1, 2020
Day 79

Vigil.

"Almighty God, grant us a quiet night and peace at the last."[4]

Earlier tonight I had a wave of extreme anxiety. After the kids went down, I wanted to know what was going on in the world, thinking it would calm my fear. I opened my laptop and surfed the news. It just made me angry and sad and even more scared.

I believe the struggle for justice is righteous and holy. I also am afraid of what might happen in the night.

I kept thinking of my people, especially those who are watching all this unfold on TV, day after day, in isolation. I yearned to gather them, to help them be less afraid and less alone.

So I closed my computer, opened my church directory, and prayed through it.

If you're a member of Peace, you can be sure that you have been prayed for tonight, along with protesters and police, presidents and peacemakers. Journalists. The neighborhood. My family. The whole world.

"Now in peace I will lie down and sleep. You alone, Oh God, make us secure."[5]

Sleep well world. God holds you.

June 2, 2020
Day 80

I've been wrestling with, *What is the right thing to do?* I have been convinced, as I shamefully wasn't before, to go all in on the anti-racist movement of this time. I am busily educating myself. Reading. Watching sermons from preachers outside my tradition. I want to do more.

In a previous life, I would be down at the protests in Washington, D.C. I know the power of someone in a clergy collar showing up. I would be aiding nearby churches, giving out water, and volunteering my time. I am impressed with the consistent, nationwide drumbeat for justice. I want to be there.

But in the "two smallish kids, husband with a full-time job, no daycare, solo pastor of a busy church in the middle of a pandemic" life, that hasn't been the right choice for me to make.

I've decided to stop asking myself, *What is the right thing to do?* and instead ask, *What is mine to do?*

What is mine to do?

The words "local" and "relationships" keep coming to mind. Today I let our ecclesial leaders know I would have their backs as they stepped out for justice. I called our police force to thank them, establish a connection, and make it clear I hoped for peaceful support of protests in our area. I led a Bible study in which we talked about authority, crucifixion, and baptismal identity. I drafted a letter to our congregation. I talked with a leader of our racial justice team.

I also played with my kids in a park and read lots of books to them. I watered my garden. I hugged my husband. This sounds like small stuff, but it's not insignificant. It is mine to do.

There may come a time in the near future when I and my collar will need to show up at a protest. I will weigh it carefully, remembering that each person protesting is putting themselves and their family at extra risk of coronavirus. That's not only from contact during a protest, but even more if they end up in jail. This stuff is real.

Tonight, Paul's first letter to the Corinthians brings me peace:

> Now there are varieties of gifts, but the same Spirit;
> and there are varieties of services, but the same Lord;
> and there are varieties of activities, but it is the same
> God who activates all of them in everyone. (1 Cor
> 12:4–6)

Sleep well world. God holds you.

June 3, 2020
Day 81

Every Wednesday during the pandemic, I've held a mid-week check-in, Bible study, and prayer. We always focus on a psalm. The Psalms have been prayed for thousands of years. They remind us that nothing we're experiencing is new. I find that comforting, even though I sometimes wonder if we're making any progress.

As I paged through Psalms today, I was again amazed again by their relevance, this time to the struggle for black lives. They speak to violence against innocents, the courage of those who take the lonely path of righteousness, the shaking of human institutions, the removal of unjust leaders, the eternity of God.

I don't have many words of my own tonight. I am tired. So I'll leave you with a choice section of Psalm 7:15–17 (MSG):

> See that man shoveling day after day,
> digging, then concealing,
> his man-trap down that lonely stretch of road?
> Go back and look again—you'll see him in it headfirst,
> legs waving in the breeze.
> That's what happens;
> mischief backfires;
> violence boomerangs.
> I'm thanking God who makes things right.
> I'm singing the fame of heaven-high God.

Sleep well world. God holds you.

June 4, 2020
Day 82

True confession: nearly every day I think, *This would be so much easier without children.* Our kids are five and three. I don't wish them away. Not at all. But being at home, doing some of the hardest work of my life, with them constantly here too is draining and sometimes impossible. It just is.

When I see the protests, my first thought is, *I'm so glad they're keeping the pressure on.*

My second thought is, *Please stay safe and wear masks.*

And my third thought is, *Who is watching your children?*

A few years ago, in one of our early discussions of racial justice, a church member apologized for needing to bring her children. I've never forgotten what another member pointed out: in movements involving women, children have always been there too, playing on the floor or nursing or napping, passed from loving arms to loving arms.

Psalm 8:2 says, "Out of the mouths of babes and infants you have founded a bulwark . . . to silence the enemy."

I need to remember to listen to my children without distraction. That's for their sake and for mine. I need the bulwark of their babble. Children are the greatest reason to be working so hard in all this. I don't want to sacrifice mine in the process.

Tomorrow is Friday or, as we call it, Mom Day. Tomorrow, I'm all theirs.

Sleep well world. God holds you.

June 7, 2020
Day 85

Liturgy.

"Liturgy holds us when we can't hold ourselves." I don't know who originally said this, but I've often repeated it. Today it struck me as particularly true.

Last Sunday was Pentecost. We had one of the most extraordinary worship services I've ever experienced. In the intervening week, protests and political backlash and coronavirus cases all reached new heights. There is, to put it mildly, a lot going on.

This Sunday, we had a quite normal service. It was unremarkably lovely, with nice hymns and a good sermon by our presiding bishop. It didn't pack the emotional punch of last week. Instead of being disappointed, I welcomed the relative uneventfulness of church today.

I know liturgical churches can sometimes seem so rote as to be boring. But in a time when everything else is swirling with change—even if much of the change is positive—a little bit of boring is OK. It did my soul well to slip into patterns that are ancient and familiar. I was soothed by the long, repetitive reading of Genesis 1 that I've heard hundreds of times.

It was good. It was good. It was good.

I connected with God and my people and was grounded by those relationships. I'm ready for another week.

Sleep well world. God holds you.

June 8, 2020
Day 86

"I should have done this a long time ago."

I have said that phrase to describe our church's COVID-19 adaptations. We should have been live-streaming worship, avoiding traffic when we could have meetings on Zoom, and developing a greater lay-led care ministry.

I have also said it to describe my awakening to the urgency of racial justice. I should have been saying—in word and in action—that black lives matter, that the injustice in our legal system is an outrage, that I have personal work to do.

I didn't do what I should have done.

I don't want to let my shame over what I did or didn't do in the past stop me from being who God is calling me to be now. I am grateful that forgiveness is real.

I hope that doesn't sound like cheap grace. The new sense of calling will exact something from me. It will not be easy but it will be worth it. People may gain their lives. I may gain my soul.

One of my favorite quotes says, "When is the best time to plant a tree? Twenty years ago. When is the next best time? Now."[6]

I repent for what I didn't do twenty years ago. And I am here. Now.

Sleep well world. God holds you.

June 9, 2020
Day 87

There's a category of words that are their own opposites. They're called "contranyms." Two common ones are *cleave*, which means both to cut apart and to join together, and *sanction*, which means both to approve and to disapprove.

I propose we add *sacrifice* to that list.

At George Floyd's funeral today, singer Ne-Yo came under criticism for saying George Floyd sacrificed himself.

As all sorts of people were quick to point out, Floyd didn't sacrifice himself.

Instead, he was sacrificed.

The difference is power. At the time of his murder, Floyd couldn't have sacrificed himself because he had no power. Instead he was sacrificed in the ancient way of killing an innocent person to appease a hungry god. Think of virgins tossed over cliffs or lambs led to slaughter. That meaning of *sacrifice* is horrifying to modern ears. Even more so when we realize it goes on right under our noses. It forces us to ask: what god are we trying to placate with our violence?

I think of the bone-chilling Bible story where God tells Abraham to lead his son Isaac to slaughter, only to stop him at the last minute. (Gen 22:1–14) Some scholars think the stoppage shows that the Judeo-Christian God does not require sacrifice of the innocent. That's a relief.

Sacrifice literally means drawing closer to God. Floyd's murder didn't draw humans closer to God; it exposed the gap between us.

I pray that I don't become so overwhelmed by that gap that I lose faith in Jesus to bridge it. He is both sides of sacrifice.

And I pray that when I'm called upon to sacrifice, I say yes. To paraphrase Martin Luther, God doesn't need my sacrifice, but my neighbors might.[7]

Sleep well world. God holds you.

June 10, 2020
Day 88

Yesterday we had the glorious opportunity to swim in a friend's backyard pool. Water relaxes me like nothing else. I wanted to swim a few laps on my own and then float on a raft, letting the worries of the world drift away. But my kids buzzing around me in their water wings weren't having it.

I made the conscious decision to focus as intensely on them as possible. To play without ceasing. This meant I was overturned from that raft by my daughters pretending to be snapping turtles, again and again and again. Then it was my turn to be a turtle, flipping them over, again and again and again.

I could tell that as we played, something shifted for the kids, especially our eldest. She relaxed and her face radiated glee. It was exactly what she needed, and to my great surprise, it was what I needed too.

It was joy.

In the midst of all the hurt, isolation, and intense struggle for justice in the world, I admit I feel sheepish about confessing such a moment of joy.

But the ability to be joyful is itself a form of resistance. Joy doesn't just come when everything is good. It springs up in the strangest moments. It comes from God, and I don't think it ever makes sense to deny it.

"Make a joyful noise unto the Lord. . . . His faithfulness is to all generations." (Ps 100:1, 5)

Sleep well world. God holds you.

June 11, 2020
Day 89

"When the sickness is over . . ."

Multiple times a day, one of my daughters starts a sentence
with those five hopeful words. "When the sickness is over,"
we'll visit our cousins and hug our grandparents and learn to
ride horses and go strawberry picking and play with our friends
and start kindergarten.

"Hope does not disappoint," wrote the apostle Paul. (Rom 5:5)
That might be true, but it's also true that hope doesn't get
fulfilled as quickly as I'd like. Hope unfolds over time, which
means it requires waiting, which is as hard for grown-ups as it
is for preschoolers.

I worry that someday the girls will stop saying, "When the
sickness is over." I don't want them to lose hope. And so I do
my part to get us to that future as soon as possible.

Pandemic hope is a mask-wearing, physically-distanced affair.
It includes cultivating a kind of patience I never knew I had. It
also involves lament. Sometimes the kids and I collectively hate
the sickness. We stomp it out, get really sad, and make lists of
what we miss. Then we get on with the day that we can have
right now, and usually that's pretty good too.

Sleep well world. God holds you.

June 14, 2020
Day 92

I preached today about the gift of conflict. Fifteen years ago, when I took the required psychological examination to become a pastor, my examiner noted that I was conflict-avoidant. I used to think that was a good thing—that being a peacemaker meant avoiding conflict—but that's not right. That's an excuse for cowardice and letting someone else do the hard work. It's also a defense mechanism, avoiding conflict to protect my own ego.

There is such a thing as peaceable conflict. That's the kind of conflict where people aren't armed for defensiveness but are disarmed in order to find the truth. I've had to learn how to do this. It does not come naturally.

I find it strange good news to discover that conflict is an expected part of Christian discipleship. When Jesus sent his disciples out to heal and cast out the demons of the time, he predicted they would not receive a warm welcome. That's putting it mildly. They were to go anyway, with no defenses except for the love of God and the truth. They were to go, disarmed for conflict and ready to bring real peace. (Mark 6:7–13)

Sleep well world. God holds you.

June 15, 2020
Day 93

I don't know what to write today. The problem isn't too little, it's too much. I've started this post twelve times, and each time, a totally different theme comes out. I need time to digest all the news. All the heartache. All the injustice and sadness and sickness and social disease. All the hopes too. All the sermons and movements and beauty all around. All of it. It's too much tonight. I am saturated.

So I'll post this prayer. It's a funeral prayer that is also prayed during compline, the service right before sleep.

> O Lord, support us all the day long, until the shadows lengthen and the evening comes, and the busy world lies hushed, and the fever of life is over, and our work is done. Then in thy mercy grant us a safe lodging, and a holy rest, and peace at the last.[8]

A cool breeze is blowing through the window. It's good sleeping weather and I'm tucking in.

Sleep well world. God holds you.

June 16, 2020
Day 94

Our neighbors had a big graduation party tonight. The music was pumping and the air smelled like barbeque. A gaggle of cousins played together.

Our kids' teary faces watched longingly over the fence from the perch of their playset. I had to explain again why we aren't playing with friends. The virus? Yep, the virus. But Mom . . . It's. Not. Fair.

Oh dear children, truer words have never been spoken. It is not fair. So much is not fair.

A Canaanite woman came to Jesus because her daughter was suffering. Jesus didn't respond at first because she wasn't the kind of person he was sent to help. She had the audacity to keep asking. She knelt before him and pleaded, "Lord, help me." Then they had a debate about what was and wasn't fair. (Matt 15:22–28)

She convinced Jesus that her daughter deserved his care. It boggles my mind that Jesus had his mind changed. He listened to this woman's case and realized she was right and he was wrong: "Right then, her daughter was healed." (Matt 15:28)

Our kids have not convinced me that their desire to play with friends is worth the risk of coronavirus, but they are right. It's not fair. Maybe there's some creative way we can give them playtime and also keep them safe. At the very least, they convinced me to give them ice cream sandwiches.

I'm raising a prayer for all the mothers who are pleading on behalf of their children. For all those who are persistent and courageous in expressing the injustices of the world. I hope I can be counted among them. I pray for all who cry, "Lord, help me," and "It's not fair," not once, but over and over again, trusting that change can come.

It's not fair. Not yet. But if Jesus can change his mind, maybe the arc of the universe really does bend toward justice.

Sleep well world. God holds you.

June 17, 2020
Day 95

I worshiped this evening at the synod's service of remembrance for the Emanuel 9, who were murdered five years ago. Five years ago, and also eight years ago and six years ago and four years ago and last month and last Friday.

The sheer numbers of horrific murders committed on "the altar of white supremacy," as the preacher tonight, the Reverend Angela Shannon, named it, is absolutely astonishing.[9]

Joined together like beads on a necklace that keeps on growing, the pattern of murderous racism has become obvious to me.

Something else is becoming clearer too: confession without action is part of the pattern. As Rev. Shannon preached, "We have been long on confession but short on repentance."[10]

Finally, the clearest thing of all is the hold that Jesus has on my heart. Jesus is more real to me than ever before too. Pieces of scripture that never made sense now make sense. The call to discipleship is more urgent. Maybe this is what Jesus was saying to the priest Nicodemus when he said he needed to be born from above. (John 3:7) I have been a Christian my whole life, but I am only beginning to understand.

Sleep well world. God holds you.

P.S. Apologies for not getting this post up until morning. I couldn't quite get this written last night.

June 18, 2020
Day 96

Once I completed a half marathon. To serious runners that's small potatoes, but to me it was a huge feat. Notice I said, "completed." I didn't actually run the whole time. For every nine minutes I ran, I walked one minute. That was the only way I could go the distance. It worked. I finished strong, and my pace was faster than if I'd run the whole thing.

This week has been hard. Emotionally, physically, and spiritually, I am tapped out. Today, my husband took the kids to a park so I could be alone in the house for two hours and recharge. That's the longest I've been alone in the house since March.

I know a lot of people think we're getting to the end of this thing, but I think we're somewhere in the exhausting middle.

I can't keep it up. At home, we're gonna figure out more childcare, give each other more time alone in a week, and take some of the pressure off. I'm making adjustments in other areas too.

The book of Hebrews says, "Let us run with perseverance the race that is set before us." (Heb 12:1)

For me, that means not going full tilt, but pacing myself so I can stay in it. It means missing some events that I hate to say "no" to so that I can give a fuller "yes" where it's needed. It means seeing all the other people in the race and remembering we're not in competition. We all win or lose together.

Sleep well world. God holds you.

June 21, 2020
Day 99

Father's Day.

I miss my dad, or Pop as we call him. He's alive and well, but he lives halfway across the country so I haven't seen him in almost a year. In many ways, I have more regular contact with him during the pandemic than before, thanks to Zoom, FaceTime and online worship. Still, I miss him more than ever.

One of my all-time favorite memories involves driving with him from Sioux Falls, South Dakota to Northern Minnesota with a boat hitched to the back of the car. We blasted Paul Simon's *Graceland* and harmonized with the Everly Brothers. I was probably thirteen years old.

The trailer popped a tire. Pop didn't worry. He knew someone would stop to help, and sure enough they did. We hitched a ride to a tiny town where a mechanic who had every spare part jammed on overstuffed shelves found the obscure tube we needed. We were on our way.

I don't know why I remember that so well. I suspect it has something to do with Pop's unshakable identity as a working class South Dakotan.

Pop lived his adult life as a lawyer and professor. Under his erudite veneer, however, there was always the salt-of-the-earth core that came from being the son of a machinist and a maid, one generation removed from the farm. Something essential in him emerged only in the rural, South Dakotan, slow-paced environment of his youth. He suddenly became interested in crop yields and fishing boats. He was with his people.

I am shaped by his early influences, for better and for worse, and there is a worse. Lurking in our history are great-great-grandparents who farmed land stolen from native people, and generations raised to "pull-yourself-up-by-your-bootstraps" without realizing that not everyone starts with boots.

This too is my history. They too are my people. They're my kids' people too, even if they never step foot in South Dakota.

On this Father's Day, I long for my kids to sit on Pop's lap and hear his old stories. They're being shaped indelibly by history in real time, but they're also shaped by the echoes of previous generations, more alive than they'll ever know.

Happy Father's Day, Pop.

Sleep well world. God holds you.

June 22, 2020
Day 100

Sometime in mid-February, schools typically celebrate the hundredth day of school. Students dress up as hundred-year olds or draw a hundred centipedes. By my count, it's our hundredth day of coronatime.

If I had a tad more free time, I would make a mobile of one hundred empty bottles of hand sanitizer or a collage of one hundred people worshiping via Zoom.

As it is, I'll just note that the scurry of a hundred days ago to "flatten the curve" and "social distance"—terms we hadn't heard before—largely worked. So much seemed undoable then. Go to the grocery store only every other week? Work without daycare? Worship and attend school online? Stay home for months? These things became doable, even if never easy.

In my first post on March 15, I wrote, "The suffering is bound to be massive, even if we stop the viral spread." Indeed, the poverty and insecurity have been devastating. Long-range economic and mental health implications are yet to be seen. Far too many people died because we did too little too late.

Still, people doing all these previously unthinkable things helped prevent an estimated 60 million infections in the U.S. alone.[11] That's no small potatoes.

We are not done yet—and the picture is far from rosy—but I think there's reason to celebrate.

Happy one hundred days! Let's keep it up.

Sleep well world. God holds you.

June 23, 2020
Day 101

At this time last summer, I was on sabbatical and about to start a pottery apprenticeship with a professional artist named Lori. I remember how nervous I was. I knew the risk she was taking by welcoming me, a stranger, into her studio. I wanted to be worthy. What if I wasn't a good enough potter to warrant her attention? What if my shiny new tools were all wrong? What if she didn't like me?

The risk of putting myself out there with Lori was rewarded. I got great pleasure in immersing myself in her artistry, I became a much better potter, and I made a friend for life.

In the gospel for Sunday, Jesus told the disciples that they may or may not be welcomed where they are headed. (Matt 10:40–42)

They took a risk going out and doing something new. The people who welcomed them took a risk too.

In these COVID days, the holy exchange of welcoming and being welcomed isn't as obvious as a stranger knocking on the door. It takes new forms. A seamstress makes a pile of masks with no assurance that recipients will like the design. Someone who hasn't been to church in years shows up at a Zoom Bible study. A person who's never been an activist joins a protest.

People are doing the soul-stretching work of doing something new for Jesus' sake. I am too. I am grateful when people welcome me in all my novice uncertainty, as Lori did, with an open heart.

Sleep well world. God holds you.

June 24, 2020
Day 102

In households across our county—and maybe the whole world—parents are asking the same question: "What are we going to do about school?" Our school board has given two options, and we have two weeks to decide.

I keep turning it over in my head, trying to figure out not only the best option for school, but also the childcare to go with it. I'm out of my depth. Everything I imagine makes me think either, *That's a recipe for infection,* or, *We don't have the energy or money for that.*

Once again, I'm asking, *How are we possibly going to do this?* But this time I have an advantage over the Sarah of 102 days ago because I've been here before. I was overwhelmed trying to figure it out way back then and yet, here we are. We made it work in large part to grace and help from others. We'll figure it out again.

Jesus told his disciples over and over that God would care for them. Something about the lilies of the field and the birds of the air. (Matt 6:28)

I can't solve the school-childcare-safety conundrum tonight, so I'm putting it down. Tomorrow will bring worries of its own. Jesus said that too. Strange good comfort.

Sleep well world. God holds you.

June 25, 2020
Day 103

Our youngest takes a long time to wind down at night, but I
know she'll soon be asleep if she asks for her blessing. I bless
her every night with the same words. She knows them so well
that she blesses her own stuffed dolls with them too. It's
adorable.

The first half comes from Sandra Boyton, of cartoon farm
animal fame. The second half, I made up.

At the end of another exhausting week, when again I have felt
the full range of emotions and dealt with too many crashing
existential concerns, a simple blessing is what I need. Maybe
you do too.

> The moon is high, the sea is deep,
> now rock and rock and rock to sleep.[12]
> God made the moon. God made the sea.
> God made you too. Sleep peacefully.

Sleep well world. God holds you.

June 28, 2020
Day 106

I'm appalled at the spike in U.S. coronavirus cases. I feel infuriated at all the people not taking this seriously. They're putting others at severe risk and dragging it out for the rest of us.

When the people of Israel were in captivity, the prophet Jeremiah suspected it would last a long time. A competing prophet said the hard times would soon be over. He did this so convincingly that it took some time for Jeremiah to realize that the optimistic version of the future wasn't trustworthy.

As he discovered the truth, Jeremiah said words that I'd like to repeat to leaders who have botched the response from day one.

"The Lord has not sent you and you made these people believe a lie." (Jer 28:15)

God's people were to be in exile for a long time. As they swallowed that reality, Jeremiah also gave them some good news. They could settle down and seek peace.

God told them, "I know the plans I have for you, to prosper you and not for your harm." (Jer 29:11)

The truth about the coronavirus, as hard as it is to accept, is better than a positive spin founded in lies.

Better yet is the promise that comes with the hard truth. God still has plans for us. God still gives us a future with hope.

Sleep well world. God holds you.

June 29, 2020
Day 107

We're celebrating some milestones in the Evangelical Lutheran Church in America (ELCA). Today is the 50th anniversary of the ordination of Reverend Beth Platz, our first woman pastor. The church broke the gender barrier then, but it took longer to break the race and sexuality barrier. This year is the 40th anniversary of the ordination of the first Black and Latina women and the 10th anniversary of the ordination of openly lesbian, bisexual and transgender women.

I have been moved all day by the pictures and stories shared by women across this denomination. Joy. Wisdom. Leadership. Power. Goodness. Kindness. Courage. Dancing. I'm so glad to be in this peculiar sisterhood. Reflecting on this anniversary, I am grateful to two groups in particular.

The first group is the trailblazers. They scrutinized scripture, prayed for wisdom, acted boldly, weathered abusive criticism, and trusted God to do a new thing. Some of their names are Beth, Jessica, Earlean, Lydia, April, Elizabeth, Phyllis, Patricia, Anita. They were the firsts.

The second group is the people who formed me in the church of my youth, a church that still doesn't ordain women. They were—and still are—cheerleaders and fierce supporters. They taught me the freedom of the gospel and to love Christ's church. Some of their names are Suzanne, Michael, Zelda, Carleton, Walter, Dorothy, Louisa, Loma.

My sister recently texted me, "You are in the right career." She's right. I am. And sometimes I am silly glad for the chance to do what I do. Thank you to all whose shoulders I stand on.

Sleep well world. God holds you.

June 30, 2020
Day 108

I went to my first PTA meeting today. Zoom, of course. The start of school in coronatime. Again, I realized just how hard it's going to be.

We will need extra help, radically rearrange schedules, and even then, our little kindergartner's first year will be a far cry from crafts and recess and a bevy of new friends arranging playdates. My response surprised me.

I feel insecure.

I don't have a well-cultivated network of parent-friends to lean on or "pod up" with. I can't take a year off of work to homeschool. We have no great options. I feel like I failed a test or lost a popularity contest. I feel like it's my fault.

This isn't rational, and it's not a cry for help exactly. It's part of the pattern of how sin often works in my life. I think I should be able to do better, even if faced with a darn near impossible situation outside of my control. I stop connecting with other people and focus on myself.

Luther described sin as "curving in on oneself."[13] My insecurity is an out-of-whack ego, a version of that inward curve made worse by societal forces pressing down, narrowing my vision so I think I have to go it alone.

Jesus lifts my chin away from myself. I see countless others who are in the same situation through no fault of their own. I see others who also need help, many of whom are in much harder situations than mine. I see the stability of Jesus' presence, giving us all a security not of our own making. I breathe and pray and trust.

"Come to me all you who are weary and carrying heavy burdens, and I will give you rest." (Matt 11:28)

Sleep well world. God holds you.

July 1, 2020
Day 109

I've been getting schooled in some history lately, including the history of five centuries of racism in the United States, the history of the 1918 Spanish Flu, and the history of political leaders betraying their people for selfish gain.

Awful aspects of history repeat themselves, weedy and persistent. I join the psalmist in crying out, "How long, O Lord. How long?" (Ps 13:1)

The answer seems to be "a long time, but not forever." Not forever, because the psalmist also says that God will outlast it all. Only God is eternal.

It makes me dare to hope that the future need not be a repeat of the past. The patterns I fear are inevitable may change, and soon. God's faithful love endures.

Sleep well world. God holds you.

July 2, 2020
Day 110

I've noticed a pattern in some of the Psalms. A long list of laments is followed by a single line of adoration that doesn't really fit. They can be paraphrased like this: "Everything is wrong; oh well, I'll praise you anyway."

Sometimes, praise comes to me naturally. But other times, my faith is tired, demoralized and hanging on by a thread. I struggle to find reasons to sing for joy.

In these times, praise is more a decision and less a natural outgrowth of my emotional state. Similar to how I sometimes have to remind myself that I love my husband (love ya honey!), I sometimes have to remind myself that I love God.

It makes me appreciate the discipline of the Christian life whereby at a certain time on a certain day, no matter how I'm feeling, I will worship.

It helps me remember that neither the state of the world nor my emotional reality determines God's character. Even when things are hard—and some days they are so hard—God is worthy to be praised.

Sleep well world. God holds you.

July 5, 2020
Day 113

My husband is out of town for a couple days. It was important for him to visit his parents. We all wished we could go, but we couldn't figure out how to do it safely. I felt unusually sad about him leaving. Our little family has been so completely together for months that it's strange to be apart.

Before I put the girls to bed, we FaceTimed with him and his parents. The girls cried afterwards. Of her own accord, our eldest took down the photo of her grandparents that hangs on their bedroom wall. She showed it to her little sister and propped it on their bookshelf so they both could see it. It calmed them down immediately.

I've been doing communion over Zoom with the church I serve. It's slightly controversial to do it this way, and I've spilled a lot of ink explaining my decision. I'm not looking for an argument here.

I'm just pointing out that my daughter's instinct to show her sister a photo of Grandma and Papa is similar to my instinct to give my people communion. I want to give as much comfort as I can. People need tangible reminders of connection. And it works. It brings us together with God even though we are apart. God is really present, even if we are not.

Sleep well world. God holds you.

July 6, 2020
Day 114

I need to go to sleep but my husband is gone and while I miss him, it's also really nice to be alone in the house. Well, I'm not technically alone. The kids are here, but they're sleeping soundly. I *feel* alone and that's a good thing.

Since the pandemic started I have had the opposite problem of those who are isolated. I am too much around people. Even the ones I love best are still people. Even the ones on Zoom are still people. I am never alone. And I am someone who loves to be alone.

I take comfort in the fact that sometimes when pressed by the bottomless needs of sick and hurting people living in a cruel society, Jesus went off by himself. I think he must have been an introvert. Or at least he knew he couldn't hear God when there were so many other voices clamoring for his attention.

I'll be glad when my husband returns tomorrow, but I'm also glad for tonight. Glad for space in the bed and sounds of a rainstorm through open windows and precious solitude.

Sleep well world. God holds you.

July 7, 2020
Day 115

One of the things I hate the most about right now is the feeling of powerlessness.

On almost every level of concern, the scope of my power is minuscule compared to the scope of the problem.

Child separations at the border plus coronavirus; could anything be more awful? I send my little money and write my little letters and post my little opinions. What else can I do? Climate change. Ditto. Racism. Coronavirus prevention. The rotting of at least a sizable portion of our country's moral core. Ditto. Ditto. Ditto.

The gospel for this Sunday is about sowing seeds. According to the gardener Jesus, it just takes one seed to germinate for the effect to be a hundredfold. (Mark 4:8)

That's hopeful. Yes. And normally the gardener in me loves to talk about planting seeds. But suggestions about tiny human actions won't cut it tonight. I'm in no mood for encouraging aphorisms like "do small things with great love," or "it mattered to that one starfish." I want big action I can see.

I call on the power of God to do what I can't. I ask boldly for the kingdom to come. I'll keep sowing my seeds and cultivating the soil of my own heart. But I look to God to bring some real change.

Sleep well world. God holds you.

July 8, 2020
Day 116

Competing needs.

I remember learning the phrase "competing needs" and feeling like I'd just been given a key to healthy relationships. That phrase unlocks me from single-minded desperation—*how will I possibly survive if you don't meet my needs right now!?*— to a roomier, more helpful set of questions.

They're questions like, *Can we start by defining each of our needs?* and, *Are they of the same scale?* If one person craves dessert while another is starving for dinner, dinner wins.

Then: *Can all these needs be met?* Usually the answer is *Yes, but not at the same time,* or *Yes, but not by the same person.* And so on.

Competing needs are everywhere right now. Well-being of teachers versus students versus parents. Health versus economy. Security for some lives versus security for others.

As helpful as I find the language of competing needs, it's even better to remember that in God's kingdom, there are no competing needs. Let me say that again.

In God's kingdom, there are no competing needs.

"You open your hand, satisfying the desire of every living thing," says the psalmist. (Ps 145:15)

Jesus told his disciples they could feed a crowd with five loaves of bread and two fish, and they did, with some left over. (Luke 9:12–17)

I admit, I often don't believe it is possible that we could have a world where I don't have to compete for what I need.

But I do believe in a God who consistently proves me wrong.

Sleep well world. God holds you.

July 9, 2020
Day 117

Nearly every day, I wander outside and end up near my flower garden. It's not intentional. I just instinctively do it. I don't water or weed. I don't even admire it, not that it's much to admire. I just kind of stand there, staring.

I don't recall doing this before the pandemic. I suspect I'm drawn outside because I need to take in a different kind of information than pixelated connection and chaotic news. Or maybe I just need a break from all the effort required throughout the day. Standing there. I do nothing but take it in. Color, light, fresh air, bees. Effortless existence. Peace.

It reminds me of lyrics from a hymn, based on a passage from Isaiah:

> Hope blooms in a weary world,
> when creatures, once forlorn, find wilderness reborn.
> Hope blooms in a weary world.
> The world in wonder echoes shalom.[14]

Sleep well world. God holds you.

July 12, 2020
Day 120

Mental health.

Last week, I heard about significantly more instances of mental illness than usual. This may just be anecdotal, but it's made me worry about the toll of coronavirus on people's mental health.

I struggled with depression for about half of my life. It affected everything. I was saved by a combination of medication, therapy, and a dog. That trinity of healers moved me so far away from the pit of despair that sometimes I can't even remember what it was like. I count that as a miracle.

I haven't had a bout of depression for a decade. I no longer take medication and the dog has moved on, but I still see a counselor biweekly, now through the teletherapy.

Although I am basically well, I benefit enormously from the counseling. All my relationships do too. Especially now, I'm grateful to have time set aside regularly to make sure I'm OK.

Jesus healed people who were possessed with demons. We don't quite know what "demons" means in contemporary terms, but it seems reasonable to think it includes conditions we now call mental illnesses. Depression. Anxiety. Bipolar. Addiction. The list goes on.

Praying tonight for all whose mental health is suffering. Praying that the savior you need will come and give you the healing that will set you free.

Sleep well world. God holds you.

July 13, 2020
Day 121

The Montgomery bus boycott, catalyzed by Rosa Parks, lasted over a year. It's not hard to imagine that some boycotters became demoralized, in roasting hot Alabama, mid-summer, some 200 days into it. They were still being viciously harassed and threatened. Undaunted, they kept organizing, encouraging each other, and pressing on. And because they were patient, it worked.

I'm trying to cultivate that kind of patience. It's not an attitude that ignores present reality, but it also knows there's no quick fix. It's a patience that shows up every day with persistent vision and willingness to keep doing what needs to be done.

In the Bible, the word that's often translated "wait" can be translated "to expect fully." I like that. I don't want a patience that waits passively. I want one that fully expects.

The Montgomery boycotters acted like they fully expected it would work, even when they had doubts.

I fully expect that this generation can heal the gaping wounds of racism. I fully expect that the spread of coronavirus can be stopped. I fully expect that the kingdom can come.

Sleep well world. God holds you.

July 14, 2020
Day 122

Immigration.

I know there's a lot going on. A lot. Along with everyone else COVID affects, immigrants and refugees are especially impacted. It's unsettling my soul.

Jesus told this story. Lazarus was a poor man who begged at the gate of a rich man. The rich man never gave him anything. They both died, and the poor man went to heaven while the rich man ended up in torment. The rich man asked for water. He was denied because he had his share of the good stuff on earth. Then he asked for his family to be warned, so they wouldn't end up in the same spot as him. Again he was denied. He was told that from the scriptures, they had all the information they needed. (Luke 16:19–31)

And so do we.

Immigration policy is complex, yes. But the message from Jesus on the topic is pretty simple. Welcome the foreigner. Do good to the person asking for help. Have compassion and kindness. Remember your own soul is at stake.

People are still begging at our door. Here are some examples of how we're currently treating them.

– A detention center for immigrants in Virginia is reported to have a 75% COVID infection rate.[15]

– This upcoming Friday, children at the border need to be released from the awful places they've been kept, but it's unclear where they will go and (as far as I can figure out) there's no guarantee they will be reunited with their parents.

– The administration wants to drastically reduce our asylum laws, making us even less hospitable for refugees from all over the world.

My faith causes me to be deeply at odds with many of my country's policies and laws regarding treatment of immigrants and refugees.

I have not used these posts to ask for an action. But I'm doing it tonight because I can't figure out how to say "God holds you" without doing something. As we've seen by the reversal of policy on international student visas, sometimes public outcries work.

The link to make a public comment on ending asylum is below. *Comments are due by the end of the day tomorrow, July 15th.

We are still alive. We have the prophets and the scriptures and Jesus. I believe we can make a difference for the Lazaruses at the gate.

Sleep well world. God holds you.

*note: in the original post, a link was included.

July 15, 2020
Day 123

Today was the deadline for our school decision. We chose to send our daughter in person two days a week and online the other two days. The other option was four days online.

This was a less excruciating decision for us than for many, but it was still a tough call on top of months of tough calls. I definitely have decision fatigue.

The psalmist wrote about having a divided heart. He prayed that God would make him wholehearted. (Ps 86:11–12) I think that's about integrity. The decision about school was so hard because my own values clashed, and there seemed to be no good options. So many of these COVID decisions are murky and divisive. The conflict isn't just between us, it's inside us.

I feel surprisingly settled about our school choice. I trust our school to teach as well and as safely as possible. I trust our kid to mask up and keep distance (it surprises me how much better these kids have mastered the basics than many adults). I also know it could all change tomorrow so I'm holding it lightly.

For now, my heart is whole and at peace. Kindergarten, here we come.

Sleep well world. God holds you.

July 16, 2020
Day 124

Hanging on by a thread. That's how I feel every time I try to connect the various elements of our online worship; or care for my kids as they melt down during a Zoom staff meeting; or tend to all the little pastoral fires that pop up in a week while also keeping my eyes on multiple societal conflagrations; or just make sure our clothes get laundered every once in a while.

I get to the end of a week and I think, well, I might not be standing firm, but I'm still hanging on.

Ecclesiastes says, "Though one may be overpowered, two can defend themselves. A cord of three strands is not quickly broken." (Eccl 4:12, NIV)

This week I met with the team that will take over all the online worship connections. A couple of neighbors helped talk through school solutions. Our kids went to three different churches' online Vacation Bible Schools. We ordered take-out. I was prayed for by name.

It may often feel like I'm hanging on by a thread, but really, I'm hanging on by a many-stranded cord. Each strand has unique skills, its own style of compassion, and a much-needed perspective. Each strand has a name. Woven together, those strands are unbreakable. God is in every fiber.

Sleep well world. God holds you.

July 19, 2020
Day 127

I'm still absorbing an incredible sermon given to Peace by guest preacher, the Reverend Yvonne Delk. Between her powerful message and all the moving accounts of John Lewis's legacy, I'm drawn to quiet reflection, not more words.

So tonight I'll say simply that Pastor Delk and John Lewis both drew a direct line from faith in Jesus to social transformation.

Courage.

This is an awful moment for our country. People of faith can meet it, with God's help, and turn it for good.

Sleep well world. God holds you.

July 20, 2020
Day 128

I came close to panicking today. I have no idea what to do with the kids in the fall. Rumors say that our School District will pull the plug on in-person learning tomorrow. I think that's the right choice, but it throws us into a new uncertain position.

Another person in my circle of care probably has coronavirus. Meanwhile the callous despots in charge of the country rage on with their science-denying, death-dealing, violent, racist lies.

I'm sad. Angry. Grieving. Messy.

But it rained. It hasn't rained for more than a week. In between the showers, we went on a family walk and splashed in puddles. The cheerful skips of our rain-booted kiddos made a delightful rhythm. It was A-OK in their world. And so in ours.

We came home, opened the windows to feel the storm raging outside, and had a good old-fashioned dance party, complete with flashlight strobes. We twirled the kids in the air to their hearts' delight. Rainwater soaked through our screens. We didn't care. We tempted fate and opened umbrellas inside the house. We grooved to Rihanna's "Umbrella, ella, ella . . . " It was hot and humid and we danced.

The Spirit helps us in our weakness. The Spirit groans with sighs too deep for words. The Spirit comes, acknowledges the mess of the world, and sets us dancing anyway.

Sleep well world. God holds you.

July 21, 2020
Day 129

The Biblical book of Romans contains a list of things that cannot separate us from the love of God in Christ Jesus. It's such a powerful balm for grief that it's often read at funerals.

I think it would be a useful spiritual exercise to come up with my own list. What casts the illusion of power but in reality can't separate us from God's love? I've written down a lot of things (a lot!) but every list I come up with sounds strident, self-righteous, and a little bit hollow.

I'm going to keep working on it. I think it's useful to name the idols, losses, and fears and then proclaim that God is more powerful than even them. Still, I keep coming back to Romans and finding comfort that no list of mine can give. Maybe that's the point.

From Romans 8:

> I'm absolutely convinced that nothing—nothing living or dead, angelic or demonic, today or tomorrow, high or low, thinkable or unthinkable—absolutely nothing can get between us and God's love. (Rom 8:38–39, MSG)

Sleep well world. God holds you.

July 22, 2020
Day 130

When coronavirus first hit, I started a Wednesday check-in and Bible Study. It's stabilized to a group of a dozen or so people who share highs and lows and pray carefully through a psalm.

Today's was a portion of Psalm 119, which is the longest book in the Bible. It's all about the blessing of God's law and the oppressive forces that try to throw us off course. It includes this line: "Direct my footsteps according to your word; let no sin rule over me." (Ps 119:133, NIV)

What a contrast to the game of crack-the-whip I feel like I'm playing most days. Up, down, losing footing, gaining traction. Ruled by all kinds of forces that bear little resemblance to God's law.

Wikipedia tells me that British abolitionist William Wilberforce recited this whole Psalm from memory when he walked home from Parliament. He learned 176 verses by heart. It shaped his days. Wilberforce led the struggle against slavery in Britain for twenty years.[16] Through the ups and downs, he kept going toward justice. I imagine he was greatly helped by this Psalm's insistence that no matter the chaos and wrong in the world, right is still right; truth is still truth; God is still God.

I want to live with a Psalm 119 kind of steadiness of faith. I don't want to be thrown around by every sharp turn. This Psalm helps me know that even if the struggles aren't over soon, I can keep walking, keep praying, keep trusting.

Steady on.

Sleep well world. God holds you.

July 23, 2020
Day 131

Exponential growth.

Unchecked, the coronavirus spreads remarkably fast. The U.S. has reported a million new cases in just the last fifteen days. That's not primarily because we're testing more, it's because we're spreading it more. It's demoralizing. After 131 days of staying isolated and being extra careful, I am angry that we are where we are, with that curve skyrocketing upward and the cases getting worse.

Scripture reminds us that it's not only devilish things like coronavirus that grow exponentially. God's kingdom does too.

Yeast. Seed. Small actions can have expansive effects for good. One prayer. One phone call. One vote. One letter. One mask. One extra beat of patience. It often seems like these things don't even make a whiff of difference, but they do. They do.

God's kingdom starts out small and hidden, but it is spreading too.

Sleep well world. God holds you.

July 26, 2020
Day 134

This afternoon the church blessed our high school graduates.

It would have been easy for this event to slip through the cracks. We only have three graduates, and everyone would have understood if we skipped it this year. I'm so glad it happened, especially since the class of 2020 missed so many other markers of this milestone.

Sunday school teachers who taught them as toddlers came out in the hot sun to celebrate at a distance. Parents gave proud, heartfelt speeches through masks. Our director of youth prayed. I read Psalm 139. One of our musicians sang the hymn "Borning Cry."[17] A handful of other stalwart church members came to cheer the kids on. One held a homemade sign that read "Peace celebrates you!"

The highlight was the presentation of homemade quilts. Our talented quilter, Kris, made one for each student. When she gave them, she described the thoughtfully chosen color and fabric of each one. They are works of art, but she doesn't want them stored away. She advised the graduates to use the quilts so much that they get ragged around the edges.

I thought of how much care and attention went into each quilt, into each life. I thought of the awesome responsibility to raise kids with faith, and how it really does take a village. I prayed for what these kids have already been through, and what their lives will be.

Sleep well world. God holds you.

July 27, 2020
Day 135

We plan to visit my parents soon, so we're in what I call "deep quarantine." That's fourteen days of even more limited contact than we normally have, and we've been quite strict. It's inconvenient as it means absolutely no childcare or trips to the grocery store. But beyond a tad more stress, the challenge of eating what we've got, and some epic messes produced by feral children, it's doable.

Back in mid-March, I asked our church administrator to quarantine for fourteen days because she'd traveled to Seattle, which was then the only coronavirus hot spot in the country. The rest of us naively thought we could remain untouched.

I remember it seemed like such a big thing to ask. By the time her two weeks were up, however, we were all at home and under no illusion we would be able to avoid the pandemic. Now fourteen days of deep quarantine seems like nothing.

Throughout scripture, people do well to understand what time they're in. Wilderness time? Resurrection time? Mourning time or rejoicing time?

To everything there is a time and a season. This is the time to hunker down. It helps that our kids understand that we're isolating so we can hug Oma and Grandpa.

If all goes well, in a few weeks our kids get to sit in my mom's lap. I'll play cribbage across the table from my dad and we'll all sing around a campfire. Can't think of a better reason to stay home now.

Sleep well world. God holds you.

July 28, 2020
Day 136

Our worship team has taken the hymn "All Are Welcome" out of rotation for the foreseeable future. The reason? The song's dominant metaphor is a building. It is a mismatch to lustily sing, "All are welcome in this place"[18] from our home sanctuaries, where, frankly, no one is welcome.

The virus has caused churches to re-examine their relationship with their buildings. And for good reason. Buildings take time, energy, and money. They easily become idols.

We keep saying, "The building is closed, but the church is active." The logical next question is: do we need a building at all?

I went to the church building today with my kids. They needed a change of scenery, or we'd all have lost our cool. They played in the nursery while I worked on my laptop across the hall. Popping in on their happy faces at play, I was reminded what a cheerful, loving space a church nursery can be.

Our building will be used next Tuesday for a community-wide COVID testing site administered by the health department. I'm so glad our church doesn't think twice about opening our building to such a community need.

Last night, I asked my daughter what place makes her think of peace and calm. She said, "the inside of a church when you're all alone." I have no idea how she knows that, but she's right.

I don't idolize the building; I know it's not synonymous with the church. But it's darn useful and sometimes even holy.

We will sing "All Are Welcome" when we return to the building. It probably won't be for a while. I look forward to that day when we are physically together to sing.

> Let us build a house where love can dwell
> and all can safely live.
> A place where saints and children
> tell how hearts learn to forgive.
> Built of hopes and dreams and visions,
> rock of faith and vault of grace.
> Here the love of Christ shall end divisions;
> All are welcome in this place.[19]

Sleep well world. God holds you.

July 29, 2020
Day 137

I often wonder, *How are other people doing this?*

This COVID time has been really hard on me, and I have it comparatively easy. My husband and I have jobs and health insurance. We are both legal U.S. citizens so we can assume societal benefits and protection of the law. We're happily married. Our kids are healthy. We can work from a home that has a yard. We can afford to pay for childcare, etc., etc.

Still it is hard. I often run through scenarios of how it could be so much harder. And I wonder, *How are people who have less even surviving?*

I write all that not to get to an answer (though the answer may be "they're not surviving"), but because there's something wrong with the question.

I can't put my finger on it, but I have a hunch my theoretical concern for how others are faring is not as holy as it first appears.

In the beatitudes, Jesus pronounces blessing on the poor, hungry, grieving and hated. He gives a warning to those who are wealthy, healthy, and laughing. (Luke 6:20–26)

I'm in the "woe to you" section of the audience. Something about not squeezing through the eye of the needle. Something about the man who gained the whole world but lost his soul.

Still, Jesus wants to save my life. Not only the lives of the theoretical poor who flit through my mind as I imagine other hardships, but mine too. I'm pretty sure our salvations are all tied up with each other.

Sleep well world. God holds you.

July 30, 2020
Day 138

America went to church today. John Lewis's funeral was a testament to the power of faith. His faith moved him to protest unjust government and then dedicate his life to make it better. Reminded of his example, I felt more hopeful for the country today than I have in a while.

In his farewell letter, Lewis wrote, "Democracy is not a state, it is an act."[20] I love that. I am grateful for a lot of what our particular democracy has enabled. I don't take for granted that as a woman, my right to vote was secured by the activism of earlier generations.

I've spent much of my life in proximity to the power of government. I served for two years in the Peace Corps. Living near Washington, D.C., I am the pastor of civil and military servants. I admire their good-heartedness and commitment. I've fantasized about running for office. I have never missed a chance to vote. You better believe I won't miss it this fall either.

But I'm not exactly a patriot. My relationship with patriotism has always been along the lines of "seek the welfare of the city to which I have sent you." (Jer 29:7)

That is, my first allegiance is to God, not to the country. Out of that allegiance, I try to create the best possible society so that all people can thrive. I care about politics not because I love the country, but because I love people.

It doesn't make sense to my understanding of Christianity that God and country would ever be put on equal footing. Jesus died at the hands of the government. John Lewis almost did too.

Lewis's funeral, his writing, his courage, his life, help me understand the proper relationship between patriotism and faith. Faith always leads. Lewis's parting words read like Scripture.

"In my life I have done all I can to demonstrate that the way of peace, the way of love and nonviolence is the more excellent way."[21]

Amen.

Sleep well world. God holds you.

August 2, 2020
Day 141

Note: I'm taking a break starting tomorrow. I'll be on vacation from work, and I've decided to pause these posts in order to recharge fully. I plan to write again on Day 162 because I don't think coronatime will be over then.

I took a coronavirus test today. I did it just to be absolutely sure that I'm not carrying the virus to my parents. I felt similarly to how I felt taking an HIV test when I taught in Namibia, fifteen years ago. I didn't have reason to think I was positive, but I was leading by example. I'd suggested my students get tested partly to make sure they didn't have it and partly to understand the emotional reasons some people resisted testing.

It's a vulnerable thing to be tested for something that comes with unwarranted shame and a possible death sentence. I felt it then. I felt it today.

Blame and its shadowy cousin shame are associated with this disease. I do think some people bear some blame for their willful disregard of science, and others for how they have almost malevolently contributed to the spread of the virus.

But most people are just trying to muddle through and stay healthy and sane. Some people have no choice but to go to work. Some parents have no choice but to send their kids to daycare. And all of us are balancing our need to stop the spread of the virus with our need to do the things that make us feel alive. We don't deserve blame, and we certainly don't deserve shame.

Jesus healed sick people. He also took away their shame.

Shaming people with the virus is counterproductive to stopping its spread. But the whispers of shame are there. For sure. They spoke so loudly in my head today that I almost didn't go to my test.

But then I told Satan to be quiet and instead listened to my own conscience, which was sighing with relief at doing the thing that needed to be done.

Sleep well world. God holds you.

SECTION 3

ORIENTING TOWARD HOPE
August 23, 2020 – December 23, 2020

"In the tender compassion of our God, the dawn from on high shall break upon us, to shine on those who dwell in darkness and the shadow of death, and to guide our feet into the way of peace." (Luke 1:78–79)

~~~

"There won't be a lot to orient the kids to as we start this year. Students will be met at drop-off points. They will walk six feet apart to our classroom. They will need to wear their masks for the whole day except during lunch. We will do everything in our power to keep the students safe, engaged and learning, but this year will not look like Kindergarten as we know it."
　　—*Personal correspondence with a teacher responding to my question, "How will orientation go?" October 20, 2020*[1]

"I feel like I didn't just get a vaccine, I got a shot of hope. It's hope that this is the beginning of the end of this terrible pandemic that we've all been experiencing."
　　—*Dr. Maggie Hagen, one of the first people to be vaccinated in the U.S., December 14, 2020*[2]

August 23, 2020
Day 162

I've been on vacation, and I feel like I've come back from a different planet. It's a nice planet. There's no Zoom there. Coronavirus is less prevalent, and you can almost forget it exists.

The highlight of the visit was five days with my parents, carefully planned so we could be mask-free and physically close.

I didn't realize how much I've been affected by the constant anxiety and diminished social interactions of the COVID life until I experienced something different. I remembered what it was like to hug my mom, play cards with my dad, and eat popcorn from a communal bowl. Our kids cuddled on their grandparents' laps for endless stories. My whole body relaxed.

On the last night with my folks, I wept. I'm always sad when a visit is over, but this was different. I did not want to go back to planet COVID.

Of course I did come back, but I'm happy to report that my life on planet COVID has changed. The visit to Minnesota recalibrated something for me, and after a week back home, it's stuck.

My anxiety is reduced. I trust the ways to stay safe more. It really helps that surface spread has been proven to be a minimal risk. I shared a bottle of wine on the back patio with neighbors and did an actual in-person hospital visit.

As I write that, I know the Sarah of two months ago would raise an eyebrow. I'd tell her I truly don't think I'm easing up on safety. But I am also taking into account that I don't have to cut out in-person social interaction at quite the levels I'd been doing before.

Being outside will be key. I plan to take advantage of good weather until it is so cold that not even a firepit can warm me up. I need to keep finding ways to be with humans, safely and relaxed, in order to be whole.

Sleep well world. God holds you.

August 24, 2020
Day 163

In the alternate universe, tonight our household would be filled with jittery excitement as we filled a new backpack and laid out a carefully chosen outfit for kindergarten's start tomorrow.

Instead we met the teachers in an online conference and we have two more weeks to wait until the virtual start. I expected to be sad but really, it was OK. It was more than OK, it was good.

I'm surprised by that. Perhaps I've just learned to accept current limitations. Perhaps I'm just aware of how relatively easy I still have it. Another black man, Jacob Blake, was just needlessly shot by a police officer. Climate change is creating fires in California and hurricanes in the Gulf of Mexico. I think I can handle the disappointment of virtual kindergarten.

That's part of it.

But it is also the promise of resurrection, the joy that comes in the morning. This is the lesson of COVID, again and again and again. We are good over here and it's not because everything around us is good. We're good because in the midst of what is wrong, God still brings joy.

One of my oldest friends texted me yesterday and said, "I hope you are filled to the brim with joy." My first thought was, *Doesn't she know we're in a pandemic?* (She's a middle school principal. Believe me, she knows!). And my next thought was, weirdly, *Yes.* Despite everything, I am filled to the brim with joy.

Sleep well world. God holds you.

August 25, 2020
Day 164

A Christian life should involve sacrifice. This ideal has been terribly misused throughout Christian history, as people without power have been lauded for making sacrifices when really they have been sacrificed.

In the gospel lesson for this week, Jesus tells his disciples about his upcoming sacrifice and they say "no." They don't understand how a man, anointed by God, who could have anything, would choose sacrifice over self-aggrandizement. And why would they? (Matt 16:21–28)

I don't understand it either. I find the instinct to self-preservation is so fundamental to my nature as to be unshakable. It rears its ugly head when I check my response to social evils against my reputation with certain people.

I'm trying to figure out what helps unlock my sacrificial impulses. The biggest key is that I am able to give sacrificially when I am not worried about my own well-being. That is, when I have enough.

The problem is one never knows if there will be enough until after it's tested.

Sacrifice is made possible by faith in this formula: those who lose their lives for Jesus' sake will find them. Learning to trust that promise is the work of a lifetime.

Sleep well world. God holds you.

August 26, 2020
Day 165

Cesearea Philippi. Tyre and Sidon. Samaria. Jerusalem. Bethlehem.

Scripture is full of place names. Usually, I gloss over them as if they aren't essential. That's a mistake. The place is always an important part of the story.

In some ways, coronavirus has erased the significance of place. All you need is the internet and you can be connected to anyone. Skip the commute and work from home. Worship with any church that's online from anywhere in the world.

When I went to Minnesota recently, I was jolted by the power of place. Their coronavirus experience was so different from mine in Virginia. Ditto their experience of racism and politics.

The national news overwhelms me. I find it helpful to think locally. What's happening on my block? Church? Neighborhood? District?

This week, church members sorted school supplies for a hundred new refugee kids in our school district. Our community gardens are bursting with food, and gardeners with neighboring plots have formed lasting friendships. A free brass concert on our church grounds elevated the spirits of anyone who happened to pass by.

My heart breaks and rages for victims of racial violence in Kenosha, and especially Jacob Blake. I fear for New Orleans and the storm beating down its door. I wonder how college towns across the country are going to stay safe.

And I know the place where God has called me. Virginia. Fairfax County. Mason District. Parklawn. Whispering Lane.

Sleep well world. God holds you.

August 27, 2020
Day 166

There are four gospels. They contradict one another and yet, taken together, they give a more complete picture than if there were just one.

In her brilliant Ted Talk, author Chimamanda Ngozi Adichie cautions against the "danger of a single story."[3] She talks about how the person telling the story has power. If all they tell is one thing, all you know is one thing. The reduction of a person to a single story is unfair, isolating, and dangerous.

Right now, I think the "single story" reigns. Either you wear a mask at all times, or you don't care about COVID. Either you think Black lives matter, or you think police are infallible. And so on. This is nonsense, of course.

In the Psalm for Sunday, Psalm 26:11, the psalmist says, "I walk in my integrity." That's another word for wholeness. He pleads with God not to lump him in with a bunch of other wicked people, but to see him for who he really is.

Isn't this what we all want? To be seen for who we are? Not to be lumped in as part of a single story but cherished for our complexity and uniqueness?

What's ironic is that the psalmist wants to be judged on his own merit and yet that's exactly what he's not doing for others. But that too is revealing. Don't we all tell unfair stories about others that may be true, but certainly aren't complete?

COVID has reduced the complexity of our communications. We have less conversation that reveals nuance and paradox.

Zoom makes it almost impossible to read body language or pick up on energetic cues. The single story is as prevalent as ever.

We are in danger of the single story causing us to miss a most important truth: God has made us to belong to each other in all our complexity. We become whole, together.

Sleep well world. God holds you.

August 30, 2020
Day 169

Today I held an "Orientation to Peace." Despite the title, it's not a primer on how to be a peaceable person, though I like the sound of that. It's part of our church's new member process. Three times a year we gather newcomers to give background on the church and help them discern membership. Usually there's a tour.

Four people attended today's session. All four were in different states. One has no plans to move here. Another has never been to our church building. They all plan to join the church.

They bonded so genuinely in the orientation that I wouldn't be surprised if they start a small group. Tears were shed.

Today we also had a farewell party for a family moving to Germany. We'll miss them, but the sorrow was tempered by the fact that they can still worship with us, at least for a while.

"Where two or three are gathered in my name," says Jesus, "I am there among them." (Matt 18:20)

I'm feeling my way through how far to stretch the "where" and the "there."

I'm sure Jesus was in our orientation today, just as I'm sure he's in our worship. Still, I like the idea of the neighborhood church. I'm not ready to give up in-person relationships as the backbone of a congregation. As much as I sense the Holy Spirit's hand in gathering our geographically-expanded church, someday, I hope to give the new members the tour.

Sleep well world. God holds you.

August 31, 2020
Day 170

Today I instituted a new annual tradition: mom-daughter lunch and backpack shopping to commemorate the start of school.

At the restaurant, we enthusiastically waved at the other masked diners from our corner on the patio, outdoors under table umbrellas, fifteen feet apart.

Our server played the role of "impressed stranger" perfectly. When our daughter proudly proclaimed she's about to start kindergarten, the server gushed, "You're so grown up!" We were in and out of Target in ten minutes, amazing considering the number of backpacks we needed to compare. Rainbows? Horses? Trolls?

We don't really need a backpack. The commute is ten feet and there's nothing to carry. But it will be strapped on and photographed on the first day.

It felt like a wonderfully human thing to do, to go to a restaurant (my first since March) and buy a school supply. I joined the company of parents everywhere wondering how their babies got so big. I grew verklempt at the thought of sending her off to school, even if it's just the next room over.

I've always been a fan of milestones and traditions, now more than ever. Rites of passage remind me that all has not gone to hell. In fact, much is still very very good.

As I spent time rejoicing in the company of one of God's lovely creatures, my own daughter, I silently thanked God for all of it.

For our waitress and our food and that little grown-up kid in a mask, deciding on the perfect backpack.

It's the one with rainbows.

Sleep well world. God holds you.

September 1, 2020
Day 171

Nearly every church I know is having disagreements over how to enact racial justice, advocate for public health, and resist an increasingly authoritarian government. It's not going to let up anytime soon.

It is strangely good news that Scripture is full of examples of conflict in church. The gospel lesson for this weekend includes directions for handling conflict in church. (Matt 18:15–20)

Communicate directly. Ask the person to listen. Try again, with witnesses to help. And try again with more people. Finally, if the person won't budge, let them go.

We have Jesus' permission to be small and faithful. Sometimes churches will splinter. Divisions may reduce our numbers. Jesus promises that two or three is enough.

I find that freeing. I have been the pastor of a church that split. It wasn't pretty, but it was necessary for the proclamation of the gospel.

On the other hand, right now, some churches, including the one I serve, have the opportunity to witness something important by trying as hard as possible to stick it out together.

We can demonstrate that Christ's love pulls people into relationships where conflict and sin can be confronted and healed through honesty, forgiveness, and grace.

Listening to one another is possible. Repairing relationships is possible. Changes of heart are possible. With God's help, we can find a lasting peace together. This too is the good news.

Sleep well world. God holds you.

September 2, 2020
Day 172

Discipline.

Coronavirus upended my daily routine. In the early days, I was on overdrive, abandoning essentials like eating and sleeping in order to move church online while also parenting young kids.

Over time, almost imperceptibly, that energy turned into confusion as my inbox became a morass of unanswered emails, reflecting the general chaos of my mind and spirit. The confusion contributed to a kind of non-clinical depression. Too often I ate bags of popcorn, yelled at my kids, skipped workouts, and stayed up late watching pointless TV.

Vacation was a major reset. Upon our return, my husband and I made a family schedule for each day. We've stuck to it, moving bedtimes up an hour and ensuring there's time in the day for exercise and family fun. I've started going back into the office, dressing professionally most days. I am also getting back into reading scripture and prayer at the start of each day.

The psalmist writes, "Teach me your lessons for living, that I may stay the course." (Ps 119:33, MSG)

As autumn begins in earnest, I have a hunch such disciplines will be more important than ever for staying focused, sane, and joyful. I'm sure I'll need a lot of grace (I'm staring at a basketful of unfolded laundry as I write that), but I hope I can stay the course that leads to life.

And now, per the schedule, I am going to bed.

Sleep well world. God holds you.

September 3, 2020
Day 173

Since Easter, I've celebrated communion via Zoom. I mention it tonight not to get into the theology of online communion but because I want to focus on the word *celebrate*. I'm in the mood for a party.

Nothing special has happened. In fact, the news of the day continues with its bleakness. But we've made it through nearly six months of pandemic, it's a holiday weekend, and I think everyone who has been through too much deserves a few days to kick back and revel.

Communion rarely feels like celebration. To be sure, it's a multilayered moment of worship where more than one thing is happening. There's forgiveness, intimacy, prayer, presence, grace, and community. People often cry at the altar, but they rarely laugh.

I hope to carry a celebratory spirit with me to the altar on Sunday and approach the feast like a party. God has brought us through some really hard stuff. High fives and cheers to you all. Praise God from whom all blessings flow. Party on.

Sleep well world. God holds you.

September 8, 2020
Day 178

In the beginning.

Our eldest started kindergarten today. She's online of course. The teachers were wonderful. She did OK. It was not great but also not awful.

Beginnings are always important. This one felt anticlimactic. It wasn't that different from the last 177 days, with us all under one roof managing schedules and meals and expectations.

Still, all day I was aware our child was starting something new. I had nervous mom-energy and had to restrain myself from popping in on her or asking too many questions during breaks.

She may be a student for the next fifteen or twenty years. They won't all be in coronatime. I hope very few of them are online. But I have no doubt that as her life unfolds, it will matter in unforeseeable ways that it started like this.

Sleep well world. God holds you.

September 9, 2020
Day 179

I find the state of the world completely overwhelming. Fires burn out of control out west, another indication that climate change is not some predicted future but a very present reality. Bob Woodward's book, *Rage*, exposes that our president betrayed his most basic responsibility to protect us when it came to the coronavirus.[4] That's just today.

I don't usually talk in terms of spiritual warfare, but the forces of evil sure seem to be winning. It strikes me as a bit lame that the best chance for good to prevail comes down to the vote, as if evil ever walks away without a fight.

Voting is critical. Yes. So is strategizing and mobilizing and protesting and throwing all the resources we can into creating ways for the power of good to prevail. At the same time, I am trying hard to plant this truth in my heart:

God can do what we cannot.

Jesus "crushed hell underfoot"[5] not because a bunch of people did what was right but despite their doing so much wrong. He did it because he was God.

Faith in Jesus is not primarily about how we determine what to do. Instead, it is about the one who frees us when "we cannot free ourselves."[6]

We have the power of a good and loving God on our side. It might not look like it right now, but we do. Still. Still. Still.

Sleep well world. God holds you.

September 10, 2020
Day 180

"It is not good that the human is alone." (Gen 2:18, CEB)[7]

Things felt surprisingly manageable this week, and I think it's because I have help. We hired a great new nanny. I call her our governess. She comes twenty hours a week to supervise kindergarten and care for our kids.

Our church is staffed with excellent people in the right positions. Our lay leaders have stepped up even more than before, and that's saying a lot. I love working with them.

My husband is a true partner. We have enough money to pay for what we need to make it work. Neighbors and friends pitch in.

God made a helper for the first person. This is so often read as a text about marriage that the basic message gets obscured.

Everyone needs help. Life is easier—and better—when you have it. Too many people right now don't have the help they need. It's making life impossible.

The word translated "helper" in Genesis is also used to describe the work of God. Indeed. Tonight I thank God for the help I have received, and I pray for all those doing too much, alone.

Sleep well world. God holds you.

September 13, 2020
Day 183

Today I preached about trust. The humans in the garden of Eden stopped trusting God above all else. Instead, they trusted that devilish voice telling them they knew better than God. (Gen 3) As if that's possible.

I recalled a time when I was in the throes of despair and a friend asked, "Don't you trust God?" My honest response was "no." Then the friend asked, "Well, do you trust me?" Yes. Yes I did. Through that friendship, I was brought back to faith.

The question, "Who do you trust" is big right now. Which candidate? Which news outlet? Whose version of the truth?

It's important, especially now, that the church be trustworthy. The crises of faith are real out there. The despair is too. I know some people wonder how to hear God. The other voices are getting too much airtime.

God is still trustworthy, but what if the best evidence is us? It's an awfully tall order. I could not trust God, nevermind embody that trust for others, without someone else doing the same for me.

Maybe that's what church is: people being trustworthy in God's name.

Tonight, I feel incredibly blessed by the people of Peace, my church. You with your solar panels and refugee welcome and faithful children and beautiful music and racial justice initiatives and good, good hearts. You all help me keep the faith.

Sleep well world. God holds you.

September 14, 2020
Day 184

I always write these posts at night, when everyone in my household is asleep and I'm winding down too. Tonight, I keep thinking of all the people carrying heavy burdens night after night, often unseen. I think of those who work at night, or cry with grief, or worry over bills, or wake up to feed newborns, or sleep in jail. This prayer from the compline service comes to mind:

> Keep watch, dear Lord, with those who work, or watch, or weep this night, and give your angels charge over those who sleep. Tend the sick, Lord Christ; give rest to the weary, bless the dying, soothe the suffering, pity the afflicted, shield the joyous; and all for your love's sake. Amen.[8]

Sleep well world. God holds you.

September 15, 2020
Day 185

Allow me to reminisce. 185 plus 3 days ago, I decided to move our church services online. I made this decision after days of deliberation, lengthy "will you or won't you?" text streams with other pastors, and hard conversations with council members.

I was supposed to get out of town with the family for a mini-vacation, but things had been so up in the air we hadn't planned where to go. After getting the proverbial ducks in a row—including testing the tech and sending the guest pastor and lay leaders detailed emails—I went away.

I remember deliberating about that decision too, justifying it, thinking, *This might be your last chance to get away for a while.* We went to the Eastern Shore of the Chesapeake Bay, rented a gorgeous Airbnb that just had a cancellation, and experienced the dissonance that has since become the everyday reality; we truly enjoyed ourselves while also dealing with the ominous feeling that everything was wrong. Over the weekend, reports rolled in. Daycare was canceled for a month. School was too. Every church was going virtual. We stocked up on groceries on the way back.

When we got home, I snuggled my kids to sleep and wrote my first post. I thought it would last a month, tops.

Tonight is the six-month anniversary of that first virtual worship service and my first post.

What was true then is even more true now. There have been inconceivable ups and downs. The logistical challenges have felt insurmountable. The sorrow has been immense. The inequalities and injustices have been exposed. The grief has been incalculable.

And always, something else too. Everything is wrong, and every day has joy.

Though I would not wish these last six months on anyone, leaning into that dissonance—that paradox—has brought me closer to God. And for that I am grateful. I know Jesus more intimately now. I honor incarnation. I see the cross in a new way. I value community in all its imperfect forms. Faith is alive.

"We are sorrowful yet always rejoicing, as poor, yet making many rich, as having nothing, and yet possessing everything." (2 Cor 6:10)

I'll keep writing.

Sleep well world. God holds you.

September 16, 2020
Day 186

I'm reading a biography of Dietrich Bonhoeffer, the German Lutheran pastor who led a faith-based resistance to Hitler and was executed in a concentration camp.[9]

I've just learned that he didn't grow up going to church regularly. Yes, he was the descendant of theologians and pastors, and his mother was an intensely faithful woman. Yes, he had family devotions and theological education at home from a young age, but the Bonhoeffer family wasn't what I'd call active in church. If they were in my church, I'd worry about their commitment.

This has given me a few insights. 1) God gets who God wants. 2) Church is important—Bonhoeffer became a profoundly committed churchman—but it's hardly the only way people are formed in faith. 3) What happens at home really matters.

Our online participation is slowing down. I sense some enthusiasm waning, starting with myself. We will do an in-person worship service outdoors this weekend, maybe a few more if it goes well. But by and large we'll be online for the bulk of our ministry for the foreseeable future.

I was getting quite blue about this, but reading about Bonhoeffer's childhood has made me less gloomy about all the church-at-home to come.

Our numbers might decrease. But it's hubris to think that has something to do with people losing faith in God. People who are checking out of church haven't abandoned God. They are just tired of Zoom meetings and virtual connections and their pastor preaching into a camera. And they're finding God in social movements and new communities and yes, in at-home devotions.

God can reach people that have nothing to do with formal church.

That might make my life's work irrelevant (though I still see plenty of reason for the church to keep plugging away), but it's also awfully freeing to remember.

If the end result is a few more Dietrich Bonhoeffers, that would be just fine.

Sleep well world. God holds you.

September 17, 2020
Day 187

I've been craving good theology lately. I even caught myself looking up degree programs, fantasizing about learning more.

There's a theological crisis afoot. It contributes to our political, environmental and health crises. Too many of my fellow Christians are proud of behaviors that are blatantly idolatrous, cruel, and just not very Jesus-y. I wonder if we worship the same God.

When the country's vice-president replaced the word "Jesus" with "Old Glory" while quoting Scripture in his speech at the Republican National Convention, some large slice of the Christian American pie revered him.[10] It sent me to a new place of dismay.

It also sent me to Bonhoeffer and Karl Barth, theological powerhouses behind the church-based resistance to Hitler. They worked with all their might to bring Christianity back from the brink of an evil alliance with facism and white supremacy.

Such work is being done by contemporary theologians, writing directly into the disastrous relationship between Christianity and racism, refugee abuse, nationalism and science-denial. I am hungry for it. For theological language to expose and replace the corrupt version of Christianity that is at least partly responsible for where we are right now.

I'm not going back to school. But I am reading more (and taking suggestions). I'm finding solace and hope in theology that keeps Christianity centered on a God I can believe in.

Sleep well world. God holds you.

September 21, 2020
Day 191

I rarely take surveys. They're always too long and feel impersonal. Since the coronavirus, though, I've taken a lot. Mostly they've been for our daughter's school. (Schools have sent so many surveys that one comedian has a joke about taking a survey about surveys.)

I've rarely given surveys either, but in the past two weeks I've sent two. Both have been about adding in-person worship back into the mix.

Heeding the feedback from survey #1, on Sunday we worshiped in person, outdoors. It was the first in-person service in over six months. I was giddy and energized. About forty people came, with the bulk of our congregation still worshiping with us online.

The first time I said, "The Lord be with you," and heard a group of people say, "And also with you," I felt almost physically jolted backward by the power of the response.

For me, the whole thing was great. But I have just sent out survey #2 because I don't really know what it was like for others.

With over half of our worshipers online, the intimate community that we formed over coronavirus was fractured. What was it like for the online worshipers? I don't know. Nor do I know what it was like for people who had to squint into the sun or wonder if all the safety measures really were enough.

It makes me think about the call and response pattern of worship.

The Lord be with you. *And also with you.*
I'm doing well, are you? *No, I'm struggling.*
I'm sorry to hear that. *Yeah, I don't know what to do.*
Lord have mercy. *Hear our prayer.*

I miss the call and response patterns of pre-COVID life. Too many emails end up in an inbox version of a black hole. Zoom is great for what it is, but I can't pick up on physical cues or uncomfortable silences.

So, surveys. And phone calls instead of emails. And taking more time to ask, "How is this going for you?" and waiting to hear a response.

Sleep well world. God holds you.

September 22, 2020
Day 192

"Search me, O God and know my heart." (Ps 139:23)

My dad had open heart surgery yesterday. All went well. It was routine, as these things go—an upgrade of valve and wall meant to gain him many more years of life.

He is fine. Recovering apace. Miracle of medicine. They can stop a heart for five hours and sew in a piece of pig and start it again and within hours, he's joking with nurses, asking for his phone.

It is simply amazing. I am bowing with gratitude for the surgeon and anesthesiologist and janitors and even that pig. I love my dad.

There is also this: two hundred thousand people have died from coronavirus in our country. Each was loved and cherished by someone. The virus was bound to take some lives, but it did not need to be this way. What a disaster. What a disgrace.

When I consider what's possible when resources and skills are mobilized so that one person can have open heart surgery, I'm even more heartsick to consider all that has gone wrong to add up to two hundred thousand.

"If I go up to the heavens you are there, and if I make my bed in Sheol you are there too." (Ps 139:8)

I sense that my gratitude and heartache are more connected than I know.

God dwells at the extremes. "Where can I flee from your presence?" (Ps 139:7) With every rejoicing family and every grieving family, with every doctor who has saved a life and every doctor who has recorded a death. In all of it, Oh Lord, you are there.

Sleep well world. God holds you.

September 23, 2020
Day 193

Black lives are sacred. In typing that, I just realized the word sacred looks a lot like scared.

The scripture this Sunday centers on the Joseph of technicolor dreamcoat fame. He is sold into slavery by his brothers. Then, years later, he has the opportunity to confront his brothers, reconcile and forgive. He does, and that's really nice. Really tidy. (Gen 37)

It is part of the problem. Too many Christians look at that story and say, "Oh how nice, Joseph forgave his brothers. Let's all get along." We go too quickly to forgiveness without considering the amount of truth and justice that precedes true reconciliation.

Joseph's brothers came to him, utterly humiliated and begging for their lives. And still Joseph tested to make sure they were honest. By that time, Joseph had power, real power, in a government. The tables had turned. Forgiveness did not happen without change. God can and does forgive anything. In human relationships, forgiveness is the key that unlocks the future. I'm very pro-forgiveness.

But tonight, and for a long time to come, it would be absolutely wrong to ask Breonna Taylor's loved ones—or anyone who has been a victim of the racism written through our justice system—to try to forgive, or get over it, or be anything but angry, sad, and scared.

Black lives are sacred.

Sleep well world. God holds you.

September 24, 2020
Day 194

"Come to me all you who are weary and burdened and I will give you rest." (Matt 11:28)

Everyone I know is struggling right now. Some have much heavier burdens than others, to be sure, but everyone is carrying some invisible load, including me. It takes energy to go about the day trying to bear it lightly and not get crushed under its weight. It is wearying.

Tonight I am imagining Jesus taking that load, like a friend helping take off my backpack after a long day of hiking. I picture him setting it down somewhere in the shadows and letting me feel the freedom and lightness of my body without that burden. It will be there to be picked up tomorrow. It might feel heavier then, or different. I will be strong enough to put it back on.

Tonight, with Jesus' help, I am putting it down. I pray you can too.

Sleep well world. God holds you.

September 27, 2020
Day 197

I preached today on the character Reuben in the Joseph story. The other brothers would have killed Joseph if not for Reuben's intervention. He stopped the murder, but his success was short-lived. The brothers sold off Joseph when Reuben wasn't there.

Upon discovering this, in anguish, Reuben asked, "Where can I turn?" (Gen 37:30) It was either get in cahoots with his deceitful brothers or be totally defenseless and alone. He fell in line and he was guilty by association.

I preached about the loneliness of knowing that the right thing to do will separate you from the rest of your tribe. I preached that a life of faith will always have moments of profound loneliness in which our souls are at stake.

I preached that we almost always get those moments wrong, the power of the group is so strong and our ability to know— much less do—the right thing is so weak.

A lot of people are facing profound loneliness, and not only because of the circumstances of our COVID lives. By trying to follow God to the best of our abilities, through pandemic, political dysfunction and racial reckoning, we have lost relationships with friends, family, neighbors, and yes, church.

I wish it weren't this way. I hold out hope for godly reconciliation to do what human efforts cannot: heal broken relationships. And I don't mean some surface-level healing, but one that works all the way to the core through truth, justice, reparation and forgiveness.

Until then, there will be loneliness. That kind of loneliness can be awful, accompanied by self-doubt and even loss of faith. It can also be holy. One is never truly alone in it. Jesus is there.

Scripture tells us that after some hard teachings, followers started peeling off the path of Jesus. Jesus asked the core disciples if they wanted to leave him too. He indicated he was willing to go it alone.

The disciples echoed the words of Reuben: "Lord, to whom can we go?" They didn't leave, at least not then. "You have the words of eternal life." (John 6:68)

Sleep well world. God holds you.

September 28, 2020
Day 198

Today is Yom Kippur, the Jewish day of atonement. It is one of the holiest days of the year, centered on begging for mercy, remembering the dead, and asking for a fresh start to the year.

I've only ever been to one Yom Kippur service. It was all in Hebrew, and I understood few of the words. I observed the rituals like a young child: sensory intake without the benefit of language or prior experience. Still I could apprehend that there was something holy going on. Through focused prayer and ancient ritual, the service conveyed God's presence to me partly because I didn't understand it.

My prayers these days are filled with sentiments I hardly understand, even if I know the words: forgiveness, mercy, atonement, suffering, memory, reconciliation, renewal. When I stop to pay attention to my soul, what I mostly hear is a groaning like Paul describes, too deep for words.

Blessed Yom Kippur. May the mysterious God who is beyond our comprehension show mercy to us all.

Sleep well world. God holds you.

September 29, 2020
Day 199

Isaiah 5:1–7.

This is a love song to God's people. We have been given all we need, made for wholeness and tended by a God who loves us dearly.

God is grieved. Our caretaker has looked for fruits of justice but found scars of violence, has looked for fruits of righteousness but seen only the tears of the oppressed.

Our God still loves us, dearly. We remain alive in this vineyard. It has not been destroyed.

This is a love song to my church. This is a love song to my country. This is a love song to the whole world.

We still have the potential to produce the fruits of peace.

Sleep well world. God holds you.

September 30, 2020
Day 200

I started writing these posts as a way to bring God's stabilizing presence to a world reeling from coronavirus. Lately, when I sit down to write, so much else dominates my thoughts that I sometimes forget we are in a pandemic.

It's important not to forget that. What we're dealing with in other existential crises would be enough   really enough— even without this virus that's kept us apart, afraid, and very sick.

A film of pandemic covers everything right now. Sometimes, on days when routines are predictable and our bubble is tight, it is hardly visible. But that might be part of the problem. It is always there, and it is exhausting and stressful in ways I don't always comprehend.

The compassionate Jesus doesn't ever pretend things are fine. He is most powerful when he acknowledges what is wrong. It helps him know how to go about loving people back into wholeness.

This has been a rough week. I almost wrote, "for no particular reason," but that's exactly wrong. For many, many particular reasons, this has been a rough week. One of them is certainly the pandemic. I do well to remember it.

Sleep well world. God holds you.

October 1, 2020
Day 201

On Thursdays, I usually write a brief email to the church I serve. Here's what I sent today:

Dear Church,

In the days and weeks ahead, our church, community and country will almost certainly face more rancor and divisiveness than we have faced in my lifetime.

I will be very glad if that prediction is wrong. Still, I am spending time preparing for it through spiritual practices like prayer, scripture study, and worship. I am also preparing with physical practices like walking, eating well, sleeping, and not overworking.

I keep coming back to this basic truth: Jesus Christ is the way. The more upset and worried I get, the more I find that time spent with Jesus calms, directs, and inspires. The more I hear falsehoods and hatred, the more I need to hear God's truth and love.

My most sincere prayer for you, these days, is not that you would get through this time unscathed. Rather it's that you would get through this time full of the courage that comes from the gospel, profoundly aware of the grace that is there for you, and faithful to the one who calls you beloved.

Be at Peace, Pastor Sarah

Sleep well world. God holds you.

October 4, 2020
Day 204

In the middle of the night Thursday, as my husband took over for me in trying to get a restless kid to settle down, he whispered in my ear, "The President has the virus."

I did not go back to sleep. In the three days since then, my thoughts have never strayed far from that reality. I wonder how he's doing; how the rest of that cadre of the sick are faring; how many other innocent people were infected by his recklessness; what it means for our country, security, and election; and on and on. It's distant and at the same time, all-consuming. Quite a few people have asked me what I think. Truthfully, I don't know how to talk about it. I don't have any words.

I was very grateful that Pastor Bob Holum, one of my mentors and a prophetic, precise, poetic preacher, was in our online pulpit today.

I needed to hear a sermon, not give one. He preached a beautiful one on grief, brokenness, common good, and our primary identity as citizens of the kin-dom of God.

I also needed the silence of a garden on a perfect fall afternoon, the music of Bach on the radio, and the laughter of my kids as they bombarded me with stuffed animals.

Words are not the only way—often not the best way—to figure out what God is saying.

Sleep well world. God holds you.

October 5, 2020
Day 205

The TV show *Madam Secretary* has been one of my go-tos during COVID. In an episode where the Secretary of State was running for President, she showed grief on the campaign trail. At first, her campaign manager worried that her breakdown would ruin her chances. Then he realized her emotions helped her connect with people. He had an about-face, saying, "Vulnerability wasn't her liability, it was her superpower."[11]

The scripture verse "Power is made perfect in weakness," (2 Cor 12:9) hung on a faded felt banner in a church I used to serve. I walked by it day after day and wondered, *What does that mean?* I still wonder.

I never expect that weakness will be associated with power, especially when I am the one who is weak. Vulnerability doesn't feel like a superpower; it usually just feels cruddy.

It's clear in the gospels. The ones who thought they were strong couldn't hear Jesus' message. They rejected his love. Meanwhile, hungry people got to eat with him. Sick people felt his touch. God showed up to those in need. And God showed up *as* one in need, one who could be hurt too.

I am comforted to remember, on a day when I have cried and raged and felt very unsure of myself, that God would not love me better if I were impervious to pain.

I am comforted to remember that Jesus did not come with a cape and shield and superpower, but with bones and flesh and a heart that could break, and that's what made him so great.

Sleep well world. God holds you.

October 6, 2020
Day 206

I've been going through some stuff. I'm trying to be faithful to the gospel and centered on Jesus. I'm trying to speak the truth that needs to be said, but always with humility and love. Like every church leader in the U.S. right now, I'm challenged to figure out how to preach, how to lead, how to pray, how to worship, how to keep people together, and how to let people come apart. It's nothing exceptional, but it is hard.

I needed a pastor. I reached out to a few I knew could help. One texted back immediately with scripture and an offer to connect as soon as possible. That simple, kind, response did my heart well. Another cleared an hour out of his busy schedule to talk. The time we spent today was exactly what I needed.

He gave me a listening presence, direction, a reflection of Jesus, truth, a new perspective, and space to be real. He also gave me three simple "rules" that he picked up from the founder of Methodism, John Wesley. I am going to tuck them in my spiritual backpocket.

In a genuine Christian community, one never has to "go through stuff" alone. Sometimes the companion is a trusted friend. Sometimes it's someone who lived three hundred years ago. Always, Jesus is there too.

The three rules:

1. Do no harm.
2. Do good.
3. Stay in love with Jesus.

Sleep well world. God holds you.

October 7, 2020
Day 207

Today in Bible Study we looked at parts of Psalm 55. It's full of the anguish, pain and betrayal that comes from the worst of human behavior. Right in the midst of cries of deep distress, the psalmist writes:

> I want some peace and quiet.
> I want a walk in the country,
> I want a cabin in the woods.
> I'm desperate for a change
> from rage and stormy weather. (Ps 55:7–8, MSG)

I love that this is in the Bible. I admit, often these days I dream of escape. I mean, who doesn't just want a break!? But the psalmist doesn't have the option to really get away. Instead, he goes deeper. He speaks honestly, then he turns to God, saying:

> Pile your troubles on God's shoulders –
> he'll carry your load, he'll help you out . . .
> I trust in you. (Ps 55:22–23, MSG)

Sleep well world. God holds you.

October 8, 2020
Day 208

I have never had a sermon done on a Thursday until today. I just finished mine because I'm participating in a pulpit share, and the other churches need it early to create their prerecorded worship services.

Over four months, four neighboring churches from different denominations will hear from one another's pastors. I'm really excited about it as a show of unity during a time of divisiveness and suspicion. They are some phenomenal pastors, and it is a unique gift of pandemic worship that we can share preaching in this way.

My sermon is on the gift of difference as a way to keep us from the sin of idolatry.

I didn't include this quote that is commonly attributed to St Augustine, but I definitely had it in mind:

"If you believe what you like in the Gospels, and reject what you don't like, it is not the gospel you believe in but yourself."[12]

And now I'm done with my sermon! Whatever will I do on Saturday night?

Sleep well world. God holds you.

October 11, 2020
Day 211

Two bouquets graced our altar today. One celebrated a baptism that took place right before the main service. The other honored two people whose ashes were to be placed in our columbarium later in the day. The baptism and interment were both lovely in their ways. Small, intimate, low-tech, and holy.

During our main worship service, however, I've never felt more disconnected.

We were originally going to have worship in person, outdoors, but it threatened to rain. So only the worship leaders came in person, and everyone else was on Zoom. We tried to have worship leaders from both formats so no one "location" had all the participation. Because it was a last-minute decision, we didn't have time to test it fully.

Our musicians sang beautifully, but there were long periods when those of us leading worship from the sanctuary really didn't know what was going on in the Zoom world. The internet was glitchy. We talked over each other. My computer froze while the baptism video was being played. I left worship feeling disappointed, demoralized, and really distant from my people. That's not how I usually feel after worship, especially when we put so much planning into it.

I want a do-over.

I can't get one, so instead I'll try to place a day like today in the context that was represented by those two bouquets.

Baptism and death.

Between baptism and death I have had a lot of days. I hope to have a lot more. God's call beckons me along that journey, and God's grace always shows up, even if I don't feel it.

Tomorrow is another day. Next week has another Sunday. There are plenty of days to sing God's praise.

Sleep well world. God holds you.

October 12, 2020
Day 212

Today is our wedding anniversary. Seven years. Last year, we spent it on a church retreat, singing, making art, reflecting on God and creativity. It's an indication of the harmony in our marriage that we loved celebrating that way.

Tonight I led a church study of Bonhoeffer. The topic was community. According to Bonhoeffer, Christ is revealed in community. Other people are essential for faith.

Bonhoeffer's no idealist. He knows the difficulty of community and he cautions against "ideal community" as a dangerous fiction. Instead, he insists on the need for authentic community, composed of real, sinful people drawn together in Christ's love.

I have found this kind of genuine community over and over again in church, including last year at the retreat. And I have certainly found it in my marriage.

Before our wedding, my bishop advised me not to forget that my most important church was the one created at the kitchen table every morning. Me and my husband. That church has expanded to include our daughters. There's no ideal here. Our marriage is real, with fights and grudges and lots of opportunities to show one another grace.

Not everyone is built for marriage. That's true. But some are. My heart breaks for people who long for marital companionship and don't have it, especially during coronatime. It breaks too for people whose marriages don't give them comfort, forgiveness, or grace.

As Bonhoeffer said,

> It is not simply to be taken for granted that the
> Christian has the privilege of living among other
> Christians . . . [their physical presence] is a source of
> incomparable joy and strength to the believer.[13]

May I never take this marriage, this kitchen table church, for
granted.

Sleep well world. God holds you.

October 13, 2020
Day 213

One of my basic problems during coronavirus is this: I don't like computers. I much prefer physical books to Kindle, paper and pen to email. I wear an analog watch. I revise my dream home renovation using graph paper, pencil, and eraser. I like to look at photos printed out, the old fashioned way.

Sometimes I stare at my laptop in the morning and know I have to open it in order to do everything else, but I just don't want to. I don't think it's because I'm a luddite or even that I'm too old to be a digital native, though that's true.

I think I just don't like it, in the same way that I don't like to listen to synthesizer music or spend all day in fluorescent light or play video games. I almost always like things that are closer to nature. It's just who I am.

I believe it's the case that some people genuinely like interacting with the world through a computer. And more, I believe that some people find that the intricacies of a computer make them adore the God who could make such a thing possible.

I'm not one of those people. Though I do marvel at what computers enable, I'm tired of being in front of a screen. It makes it hard some days to live this COVID life. I don't have any great meaning to draw from this. Just claiming it. And now I'm going to turn off my phone, drink a cup of tea from a handmade mug, light a candle, and crack open my novel.

Sleep well world. God holds you.

October 14, 2020
Day 214

I am having difficulty concentrating. I'm supposed to be making plans for November and December, Advent and Christmas. Instead I can't think past November 3.

I'm keyed up about the election, and not in a good way. I'm constantly aware of the big "what ifs" hanging in the air. "Who are you for?" underlies every human interaction. As it draws closer, the election buzz in the back of my mind grows louder.

It's a very big deal, and I'm definitely in the camp that says there's a political aspect to the life of faith. But I am also certain that it isn't the only thing or even the main thing. God is God is God.

The Psalm today was 124. It was likely prayed by pilgrims on their way to festivals in Jerusalem. It recounts the saving acts of God, including from political oppression. God is on the side of the people desperate to be released from angry, rageful enemies. Reading it, I assume that God is on my side which, of course, is something we all believe, and half of us are wrong.

Instead of assuming God is on my side, I want to ask how I can be on God's side. The words of Psalm 124 can be seen as a prayer for whoever God sees is in need of salvation, for whoever is trapped in the fowler's snare, not only to be set free, but for the whole darn thing to be broken.

"Praise be to God. Who has not let us be torn by their teeth . . . our help comes from the Lord." (Ps 124:6, NIV)

Sleep well world. God holds you.

October 15, 2020
Day 215

I've been terribly disorganized lately. I'm never someone with a clean desk or zeroed-out inbox, but the last few months have taken it to a new level. I understand why. The added stress and lack of consistent rhythm make it hard to structure the day. Plus, because I am caring for my kids more than before the coronavirus, I simply have much less time to do organizational maintenance. I understand it, but it doesn't make me feel any better.

This week, because I'm not preparing a sermon for the weekend, I dedicated blocks of time to organizing. I got to the bottom of some piles. I worked through a backlog of emails. I wrote long-overdue thank you notes. I also discovered that a reporting deadline I was having serious anxiety about missing isn't for another year. Talk about grace!

Scripture describes beauty in both wilderness and civilization. God is in the wild, the chaos, the unkempt. But God is also in cities, organization, and structure. There's something essential in both.

I know that when I am disorganized, my ministry suffers. I don't always perceive that my spirit suffers too, but it does.

Tonight, I will go to bed calmer than I was all week for having a few things checked off my to-do list. The world out there might be all chaos, but at least there's one little corner of my desk that's clean.

Sleep well world. God holds you.

October 19, 2020
Day 219

We visited my husband's family last weekend. They're south of Charlotte, North Carolina, an eight-hour drive away. We hadn't seen them since Christmas and figured we could minimize risk if we visited when the weather was still warm enough to spend most of our time outside. There were a few cracks in our COVID-prevention plan, but the time spent with family outweighed the risks. Our kids wore masks inside for hours without complaint, and I stuck to my basic pandemic litmus test: *If I found out I was exposed, would I be certain I hadn't passed it on?* I'm 99% confident in my ability to say, *Yes.*

One of the big risks was the hotel. We stayed at a major chain that had a stated policy of mask-wearing by staff and guests in all public places. The signage was impossible to miss. "Mask Required" messages were posted on all the doors and lobby windows. A poster saying, "A mask is required to enter," was prominently displayed on a stand inside the double doors. A little placard by the coffee station read, "Please wear a mask at all times in the lobby."

You can see where this was going. Ninety percent of guests I saw were not wearing masks. I was infuriated and also fairly powerless. My husband calmly asked the front desk about it, and the staff reported that their corporate offices said they couldn't enforce the rules. We had a feeling it would be no better anywhere else in town. Our strategy was just to avoid the lobby and stay away from the crowds. That was easy to do.

It was less easy to figure out what to do with my anger. It felt like road rage feels. Flashing and intense. Someone had my family's well-being in their hands and blatantly flaunted the social contract that says, "If we all follow the rules, no one will get hurt."

I can get very smug and spout off some good theology about how the non-mask-wearing half of our population is blaspheming if they use words like "Christian liberty" as their excuse.

What I'm not sure about is the spiritual disposition—mine—that will help. I know how to keep me and my family safe; I don't know how to spiritually stay in a position that's useful and Christian in the best sense of the word. I don't know what to do with my anger.

I want to stay nonjudgmental and keep in mind that there are always things about another person's decisions that I certainly don't understand. I am unwilling to discount half the country as mean-spirited, selfish people. It helps to remember that my decision to go to North Carolina in the first place could be judged by some as a risk they'd deem irresponsible. We're all drawing our own lines.

I also want to stay in a stance of listening and good humor, though it's hard to make a joke when the people lingering between me and my morning caffeine are breathing all over the communal coffee pot, in clear violation of the sign just inches from their hands.

I guess this is a place of prayer. And a reminder to bring my own coffee next time.

Sleep well world. God holds you.

October 20, 2020
Day 220

I reviewed the songs for Reformation Sunday and read the lyrics of Martin Luther's famous hymn, "A Mighty Fortress Is Our God."

I admit, I've never loved this hymn. I'm put off by the dominant metaphor of God as a fortress. I don't generally like war images in church. The melody doesn't really do anything for me either.

This year, however, I can't wait to sing it. That's partly because all this uncertainty has turned me gooey about rituals. For a lifelong Lutheran like me, there's some great comfort in singing along with those big, familiar chords.

But more, I understand this song in a way I didn't before. The protection of God doesn't beckon us to hide, but gives us courage to hope. Jesus (the "little word") isn't just passively on the side of the downtrodden, he's actively breaking the cruel oppressor's rod. He doesn't fight with weapons of warfare, but weapons of the spirit. Those weapons aren't really weapons. They are love and forgiveness and righteousness and truth. Even if we lose, we cannot lose. The kingdom's ours forever.

> Let this world's tyrant rage; in battle we'll engage!
> His might is doomed to fail;
> God's judgment must prevail.
> One little word subdues him.[14]

Sleep well world. God holds you.

October 21, 2020
Day 221

Numbers. So many numbers. Cases per day. Poll results. Proposed stimulus dollars. Recommended social distance. The mathematics of hope. The calculus of despair.

The number stuck in my mind tonight is 545. That's the number of kids whose parents the U.S. government can't find. We separated thousands of families at the border three years ago, and now we can't reconnect 545 of them. This is a special kind of horror. Almost unimaginable.

This number, 545, undoes me tonight partly because I am a parent of young kids. I can feel the terror and imagine the cries. And I bear some responsibility. It happened on my watch as an adult citizen of this country, as a Christian.

It's also nothing new. For centuries—forever—some families have been protected, and others have been casually destroyed. This is a recurring nightmare, replayed through history, to other people's kids on other grown-ups' watch. This number is so much bigger than this number.

No human is a number. No life can be reduced to a hash mark in a body count or a statistic in a newspaper report. Each one is "precious in God's sight." (Isa 43:4) That's where we start.

> Jesus loves the little children,
> All the children of the world.
> Every child in every land,
> Jesus holds them in his hand.
> Jesus loves the little children of the world.

Sleep well world. God holds you.

October 22, 2020
Day 222

Breath prayer is a classic way to pray. Wherever you are, you can bring to mind a phrase with two parts. You breathe in with one part, breathe out with the other, and repeat.

I learned it using a line from Psalm 46:10, the Psalm for this Sunday.

(Breathe in) "Be still."

(Breathe out) "And know."

(Breathe in) "Be still."

(Breathe out) "And know."

Repeat.

Repeat.

Repeat.

Sleep well world. God holds you.

October 26, 2020
Day 226

Voting.

Today my husband and I arranged childcare, walked three blocks to the Government Center, and slowly snaked our way through a labyrinth of hallways to the sacred core: the voting room.

The room was hallowed, hushed, as people imagined the future, marked their ballots, and fed their hopes into a machine to be counted.

Voting felt like prayer today, with all its solemnity and also all its joy.

I felt the release of the act. I may have actually danced out of the polling room. There was a spring in my step as we walked back out past all the people waiting patiently for their turn. I took the obligatory "I voted" photo. I was smiling big under my mask.

My vote has been cast. That work, at least, is done. Now, we wait.

Sleep well world. God holds you.

October 27, 2020
Day 227

Blessed be.

Jesus took his disciples away from a clamoring crowd, sat them down, and gave them one of his most important lessons. People they had no earthly reason to think were favored by God were, in fact, blessed.

The poor in spirit. The meek. The merciful. Those seeking justice. Those waging peace. Those mourning the dead.

These are the Beatitudes. (Matt 5) A simple statement of fact about who is blessed.

Tonight my Facebook feed is erupting with people wondering what the change in the Supreme Court might mean for voting rights, marriage rights, civil rights. The concern is justified.

Civil society may or may not change its mind about the legality of same-sex marriage. It may or may not dole out citizenship rights fairly. These things matter. Truly.

But the laws of civil society don't have any bearing on the blessing that God confers.

That blessedness can never be taken away. That blessedness will surprise you every time.

Sleep well world. God holds you.

October 28, 2020
Day 228

I am dealing with the proverbial dry well. I can't come up with much to write. I can't come up with the new ideas I need for worship and church life.

I can't get worried about increased COVID rates. I can't find much anxiety about the election. I can't muster outrage at another unjust police killing of a black man. I'm weirdly unemotional about my daughter's impending return to school. Heck, I can't even get excited about Halloween.

Burnout? Acedia? Fatigue? Change of seasons? Circadian cues to start the hibernating half of the year? Yes, yes, yes, yes, and yes.

I wonder how Jesus dealt with such times. I'm betting he never admonished himself for not being able to push through. I notice the number of times he got away from crowds, prayed alone, took a few people aside, and ate with a small group of friends. He didn't respond to everyone's needs. He sometimes was very disappointing.

I am sure that God will make a shift sometime, somehow in my energy. My verve will return. Until then I will keep moving forward as I can, pause when I need to, and find a whole lot of grace in each day.

Sleep well world. God holds you.

October 29, 2020
Day 229

The church I serve put together a booklet called *Prayers for a Pandemic*. Nearly seventy people contributed favorite scriptures, poems, art, music, prayers, and reflections. Most contributions were created during the pandemic. It's varied and simple and beautiful.

It's available online, but we also sent a physical copy of it to our members. The money and time it took to mail it may have been misspent. I know that many will quickly end up in the recycling bin.

With so little tangible connection available to us though, I wanted to get it into people's actual hands.

I picture someone keeping it on a nightstand for a while, connecting to friends' words and God's presence when the buzzing world has been turned off. I picture someone finding it in a stack of magazines in a few weeks, and at just the right time, reading the inspiration they need. I picture someone discovering it in a box in twenty years and—absorbed by leafing through it—remembering what we went through, how God was faithful.

Sleep well world. God holds you.

November 1, 2020
Day 232

All Saints Day.

In my sermon today I recounted the first time I was asked to bless someone. I was a new pastor, visiting friends who had just had a baby. The dad, a Catholic, asked if I was going to bless their child, telling me that priests do that when they visit newborns. It hadn't occurred to me that I wasn't just visiting as a friend, I was also a pastor now. It hadn't occurred to me that "conferring blessing" was something I did.

I blessed the child with words that sprang to mind. I think they came from God.

"God made you, loves you, and is always with you. Jesus is your friend."

Blessing has become one of my favorite acts as a pastor. I think of it as infusing people with God's love. I don't think the act of blessing should be reserved for professional Christians. I think Jesus gave his disciples the Beatitudes (Matt 5) partly so we'd know that part of every Christian's job description is to pronounce blessedness on people who might not ever know it otherwise.

I encouraged the congregation to be lavish in acts of blessing this upcoming week, to be generous in spreading appreciation and gratitude, and to tell someone who might not expect it that they had been a blessing.

Sleep well world. God holds you.

November 2, 2020
Day 233

"Teach us to number our days." (Ps 90:12)

Since the coronavirus shutdown began, I've been writing these posts by counting up the days. By my count we're at 233.

Since sometime midsummer, in anticipation of the election, my brother has been writing a political blog, counting down the days. By his count, we're at 1.

Tomorrow is Election Day in the United States. The votes will be all cast, if not all counted. I'm tempted to make, perhaps, too big a deal about the day. It is just a day. But it is also a frightfully important one for the future of our country. It is day zero.

I want to declare victory so we can toss celebratory confetti, call it history, and start cleaning up the mess.

And not just for our political life, but for our pandemic life and our community life too. I want an end to sickness and hatred and division. I want to go back, if not to normal, then to something better than this. No. That's not right. I want to go forward to a bright and glorious future.

I want a new day.

Tomorrow may bring something to an end in our country, but it will not all be over. My coronavirus post tomorrow will be 234, and the next day I'll add one more.

And that next day, my daughter will turn four. And we will celebrate her bright and glorious life, no matter the outcome of the election. And on and on we go.

Scripture doesn't say just one clear thing about how God works in time. It admonishes us to be alert and also patient. It describes rejoicing and also groaning. Something gets completed, something else remains undone.

The day of the Lord is like ten thousand days.

The day of the Lord is coming.

The day of the Lord is at hand.

Sleep well world. God holds you.

November 3, 2020
Day 234

Election Day.

November 3rd, 2016, four years ago, I was getting ready to have a baby. I needed a C-section so barring early labor, the birth date was scheduled for the next morning. We knew that our life was about to change. We also knew that we already loved that kid, that God would get us through whatever happened, and that we should probably get some sleep.

I can viscerally recall the combination of excitement, calm, and anxiety of that night. I remember sensing God drawing near in the waiting time.

The circumstances are very different, but tonight something feels similar. It's the waiting. The wondering. The deep-seated hope mingling with fear. And all of it essentially out of my hands.

I'm keeping an eye on election returns and wrapping presents while my husband paints a big "Happy Birthday" sign to hang from our front trees. I'm focusing on making tomorrow fun for our little kid. I'm praying.

A lyric from Dietrich Bonhoeffer is running through my mind. It's good company while I wait.

> By gracious powers lovingly surrounded,
> with patience we'll endure, let come what may.
> God is with us at night and in the morning
> and certainly on every future day.[15]

Sleep well world. God holds you.

November 4, 2020
Day 235

It doesn't take much reading of the Bible to realize that everything has happened before.

Scripture records the same anguishes that I experience. The same joys too. The same powerful despots, the same humble prophets, the same fractured communities, the same reconciliations. It's all so familiar. The scale may be different (think climate change, pandemic). But then again, it might not be (think Noah's flood, plagues.).

With both texts I studied this week, Jonah and Psalm 70, I thought, *Wow, this could have been written today*. I'm not sure if this is comforting or disquieting. On the one hand, it's reassuring that we've gotten through such hard times before. On the other hand, it would be nice to make some progress.

Today for our daughter's birthday, we did almost the same COVID-esqe celebration we did for her sister six months ago. Preparing for it, I had a sense of déjà vu that, frankly, took a lot of shine off of the experience. What once was thrilling was now just part of a tired routine.

But not for her. Today was her only golden birthday: four on the fourth. Today was her only chance to board a scooter decorated with streamers and lead the family birthday parade down the block. It was her turn to be the star of the extended family's Zoom. She was special. She loved it. And I did too.

There is nothing new under the sun. Also, we've never been here before. Happy Birthday dear girl.

Sleep well world. God holds you.

November 6, 2020
Day 236

"Jonah sat down . . . waiting to see what would become of the city." (Jonah 4:5)

At God's insistence, after being saved by that big fish, Jonah went to Ninevah. It was a violent and godless city. Jonah proclaimed that the citizens had to repent, or they would be overthrown. To his surprise, they changed their ways. Their future was secure.

Instead of rejoicing, Jonah was resentful. He went away from the city, made himself a little shelter, and plopped down to see what would happen next.

I'm writing this early Friday morning instead of Thursday night because I fell asleep on the couch and stumbled to bed late.

I was up, waiting to see what would become of the country. The votes have not all been counted. The election has not yet been decided. We are still waiting.

The same God who saved Jonah with the fish also saved his enemies from their destruction.

There is no sitting outside the system, waiting to see what will happen to those other people. There are no "other people."

There is only us. And I hold fast to the faith that God finds ways to save us all.

Sleep well world. God holds you.

November 10, 2020
Day 241

There's been lots of news since my last post. A president-elect and successful vaccine trials top the list.

Meanwhile, I got to go away to a cabin in the woods overnight by myself. It was my request for my birthday.

I love my people, but I needed to be alone. My body needed to rest and let the rhythm of falling leaves and hammering woodpeckers and crackling fire replace the rapidly cycling emotions of the last couple of weeks.

In many ways I've come this far through the pandemic unscathed. I haven't lost anyone extremely close. No one in my family has gotten sick. I still have work. My kids are happy.

But I have been damaged. This hit me powerfully, as I sat nestled on an outcrop of rocks just watching the sun on the autumn leaves. I am more affected than I probably know.

This admission is not a cry for help. Quite the opposite.

It is a byproduct of trusting that help is on its way.

Like a lost kid who keeps a brave face until she sees her mom, and only then bursts into tears, I think I can finally let down some of the defenses that have kept me going thus far.

I praised God as my brokenness rose to my consciousness. I was struck by something like relief. I was aware of God's unwavering presence. I put my hands on the rocks that held me and felt a deep and healing peace.

"Then Samuel took a stone . . . and named it Ebenezer; for he said, 'Thus far the Lord has helped us.'" (1 Sam 7:12)

Sleep well world. God holds you.

November 11, 2020
Day 242

Today is my forty-sixth birthday. I spent it quietly at home, trying to work while also supervising virtual Kindergarten and caring for our four-year old. In other words, not working. I cleaned up a lot of messes. I played Go Fish. I don't know where the time went.

"Our days may come to seventy years, or eighty if our strength remains," says Psalm 90:20.

Amy Ray of the Indigo Girls put it this way: "Half of my life is gone for sure. The other half, God willing, occurs."[16]

I tried to go hiking yesterday. I'd only gone ten minutes before I heard the crack of a rifle. I realized it might be deer season, and I look kind of like a deer. I hustled back. That's not how I want to go.

COVID-19 isn't either, if I can help it. The numbers are on the rise. There are a lot of selfless reasons to wear masks, stay home and steady on. But I admit, part of my drive to be as safe as possible is that I love being alive.

I'm not at all afraid of death. But wow, do I hope it doesn't come for a while. I thank God for the life I've had, every minute of these forty-six years, and for all the days to come.

Sleep well world. God holds you.

November 13, 2020
Day 244

I have COVID whiplash. On the one hand, life feels normal-ish. I go to stores and the office, masked and distanced of course, but still I'm out there. My kid starts in-person school soon. Sober scientists are now giving actual dates for when a vaccine could be widely available.

On the other hand, numbers are on the rise, hospitals are overwhelmed, states are re-mandating mask laws, Thanksgiving plans are being scrapped, and we may be headed into the hardest times of all.

First Thessalonians was written to people who thought Jesus would return soon, but they didn't know exactly when. Their brand of hope was alert and open-eyed, confident in salvation without being complacent about what was required of them. In the waiting time, they were given this instruction:

> Speak encouraging words to one another. Build up hope so you'll all be together in this, no one left out, no one left behind. I know you're already doing this; just keep on doing it. (1 Thessalonians 5:10–11, MSG)

These words calm my whiplash. Build others up. Encourage and be encouraged. Trust God's salvation. Keep on doing it.

Sleep well world. God holds you.

November 15, 2020
Day 246

Call me a gamer. Tonight, for the first time in my adult life, I played an entire video game.

It came about because of Confirmation Class. Three churches combine our classes once a month. We've been doing this since before the pandemic and now, of course, we meet on Zoom. Today I could not get the group to say anything. My attempts at screen sharing didn't work, and most of the kids kept their cameras off so I felt like I was teaching into a void. I was frustrated.

At the end of the session, one of the kids set up an "Among Us" game. They suddenly got energized. I logged off but one of the other pastors stayed on to play. She saids the kids enjoyed it and opened up. She offered to teach the rest of the adults. So we met tonight online. And it was fun. Actual, real, fun.

It was social in a way I've been craving. I met new people, laughed, and was entirely un-serious for an hour.

I don't think my career as a gamer will be long-lasting, but at least I have some clue what the kids are talking about. I see the appeal, especially as a way to be social during the pandemic. I'm not as intimidated by the wide world of gamer culture as I was just a few hours ago.

It's empowering to learn something new, even if it's just how to avoid being caught as an imposter Teletubby-esque alien aboard a spaceship. And goodness knows, we can all use a little more fun right now.

Sleep well world. God holds you.

November 16, 2020
Day 247

This morning in online school, my kindergartner was shown the inside of the classroom where she was slated to start in person tomorrow. Miniature desks were distanced inside quadrants of tape on the floor. The tape was arranged to look like little homes. It was cute.

They kept calling it "return to school" but for kindergartners, it wasn't "return." It was the first time.

I planned to give her a new haircut this afternoon. She was assembling her backpack and picking out an outfit.

Silly hopefulness.

At 2:00 p.m. we got the news that they were postponing. Again. The virus surge has been too strong.

It makes sense. It's the right decision. But boy, am I sad. For weeks I'd been eyeing the numbers, hedging my bets. When we got through the weekend with no big closure announcement, I went full on into hope, and I passed that hopefulness on to my child.

Scripture promises that "hope does not disappoint." (Rom 5:5)

In the short term, that's not true. Hopes are often disappointed. Just ask my daughter. The school supplies are back on the shelf. The backpack is hung up. With reluctant acceptance, we plugged the computer in for tomorrow.

Someday my kid will understand that she was part of the great communal sacrifice to keep people healthy and alive. Someday,

I pray, this disappointment will be part of what makes her able to persevere with patience, suffer with grace, and display a character that glorifies God.

Tonight, however, we are crying.

Sleep well world. God holds you.

November 17, 2020
Day 248

Sometimes I'm amazed at just how much change we've all undertaken in the past nine months. No wonder everyone is frazzled.

For all the change that's behind us, there's even more ahead. The pandemic plus the election has exposed this, if it weren't already obvious. Racism. Poverty. Sickness. Political distrust. Climate. Now's not the time to stop changing.

Lately, my reaction to the idea of another change is, *No. No more!* I want to stabilize for a while first.

On a day like today, though, I get a whiff of what the future could look like, and I'm energized for change. I started to envision worship with a permanent online component. I heard a first-hand account of the trauma of racism and got inspired to keep pressing for change. I studied scripture with thirteen-year-olds and realized our Zoom confirmation class is more effective than the old model. I met with climate change activists to expand our work.

"I will make a new covenant," said God to a people who were nearly destroyed. (Jer 31:31) I notice the "I" making the covenant is God, not me. That's a relief. That's a grace. And listen to these changes: "They will be like a well-watered garden . . . Sorrow will be no more . . . I will forgive their iniquity." (Jer 31)

Those are the gifts of God. To that kind of change I say, *Bring it on.*

Sleep well world. God holds you.

November 18, 2020
Day 249

"Let us come into God's presence with thanksgiving," says Psalm 95:2. Like many Psalms, it was likely written for a worship service, maybe to be used while people were entering the temple.

Reflecting on this psalm, our Bible study group talked about the connection between "presence" and "place."

In an email today, I wrote, "I'm here for you." Geographically, nothing could be farther from the truth. But I am. Somehow.

It's a marvel that we can come into God's presence without leaving our homes. It is true and real worship when we all show up on Zoom screens and come together.

It's not the same as being together in the same place. Something is lost. Something might be gained.

My hunch is that at the end of all this, I'll be even more convinced that people can be spiritually present to one another and to God, without being in the same place.

At the same time, I think being physically together will matter more than ever. Sure, I look forward to Zoom calls with family on Thanksgiving Day, but I can't wait for that day when we can all sit down at the table together again.

Sleep well world. God holds you.

November 19, 2020
Day 250

I took our four-year-old to the doctor today for her annual check-up. She got vaccinations: polio, measles, mumps. She squirmed in my arms as I held her tight for the shots. It wasn't fun, but the pain is worth it.

The news of a potential coronavirus vaccine is a light at the end of the tunnel, but it doesn't mean we're through. COVID has claimed the lives of 250,000 people in our country. That's 1,000 for every day since we started. That's enormous. The next few months will certainly bring that number much higher.

I want to be done. I want a boisterous Thanksgiving dinner and Christmas Eve candlelight services and to hug my parents. I want no more deaths. I wish we could all get vaccinated right now and move on. But we're not there yet.

Romans 8:25 says, "If we hope for what we do not see, we wait for it with patience."

I'm working on patience. It's active and painful. Squirmy and teary and brave. Every day.

Today it was especially hard. No reason. I just want to be done.

Patience. I need it. It might be a long wait till we're really out of the tunnel. Two hundred fifty thousand and counting.

Sleep well world. God holds you.

November 22, 2020
Day 253

Christ the King Sunday.

The scripture today was Jeremiah 36, in which an evil king tried to destroy God's word by ripping it into pieces and burning it.

The king failed in his attempt to eliminate the news he didn't like. God simply told Jeremiah to write another scroll. He did, and the book that bears his name is the longest one in the Bible. The word endured.

I think this is a basic part of the Christian message. The word endures. God's power is always at work, even when it seems like it has disappeared. Jesus' spirit rises again and again and again.

I am seeing too many people denying the truth right now. Truth about the election. Truth about the virus. Truth about the kind of sin in which we all live, from which we all need saving. I am also seeing too many people putting all their chips in political baskets, as if our politics alone will save us.

The kingship of Jesus stands in contrast to all the other ways power is held and brokered. It's enacted through love, truth, and sacrifice. It's humble and appears foolish. It gives itself away in community. It's tempting to say it's something to aspire to, but that's not quite right. Instead, it's something to trust.

God's powerful love can be denied, but it can never be destroyed.

Sleep well world. God holds you.

November 23, 2020
Day 254

Judgment.

Throughout the pandemic, there have been ample opportunities to judge other people's behavior. We're all drawing lines, calculating risk differently, and being somewhat irrational.

Now, with Thanksgiving week colliding with record numbers of cases, judgment is on the rise too.

I have a sense of righteous judgment about some behaviors. People are sick. Our healthcare system is overwhelmed. Put on a mask and keep your distance!

But with Thanksgiving, I don't think it's as clear cut as I sometimes make it. Some people are hitting emotional lows for which being hugged by people they love is the only antidote. Some haven't held grandchildren or eaten a meal with another person for nine months. This stuff is real. I understand why people are trying to figure out ways to be safe *and* be together.

"With the same judgment you have given, you will be judged," said Jesus. (Matt 7:2) He was commending humble integrity as he built a trustworthy new community of followers.

Judgment without love rips apart communities. It is toxic. I have appreciated when people approach my decisions with an effort to understand before passing judgment. I pray for the humility to do the same.

Sleep well world. God holds you.

November 24, 2020
Day 255

I develop new routines quickly these days. It only takes a day or two to establish a pattern. Then I rely on it, until it changes again. Food prep. Exercise. Work schedule. Division of household chores. Micro-routines keep me calm and moving through the day.

I've led two different Bible studies this week on Daniel in the lion's den. Both groups keyed in on the same little detail: in the lead up to his arrest, Daniel prayed three times a day, every day. This was the sign of his faithfulness.

It's easy for me to see Biblical characters as two-dimensional, as if a prayer routine just came easy. I'm betting Daniel wasn't always feeling it. I'm betting he didn't always have the time.

The yo-yo-ing demands of life right now mean I can't develop long-standing patterns of prayer. This is part of why I'm grateful for church. Weekly worship. Regular Bible studies. Daily devotions. It's so much easier to develop the routines that sustain a faithful life when I'm not doing it alone.

Sleep well world. God holds you.

November 25, 2020
Day 256

Thanksgiving Eve.

A week ago, I pre-ordered Thanksgiving dinner from a restaurant. With a vegetarian husband and picky young eaters, I figured my joy of cooking would be diminished by uneaten food and piles of dishes. Plus, I was just too sad to think about preparing a meal.

Today, I went to the grocery store and was drawn in by the variety of the produce, the breads, the beans. It gave me great pleasure. I bought the makings for some of my favorite meals. Minestrone soup. Salmon. Quiche. When I finish this post, I'm going to make the dough for caramel rolls, using my grandma's recipe. I'll finish them with the girls in the morning. The smell alone will be worth it.

Food has spiritual power to give comfort and convey love. A good meal is about much more than nutrition.

Tonight, I'm aware of what's lost for all the people anticipating pared-down dinners for their pandemic Thanksgiving. I'm aware too of the masses who can't afford good food and are on the brink of despair.

I think of all the meals Jesus ate, noteworthy because of his companions and his teachings. I wonder what the food smelled like, how the tables were set, and how much care went into the preparation. I bet they were delicious.

Sleep well world. God holds you.

November 29, 2020
Day 260

Advent.

Some of my most vivid childhood memories are from Advent.
Every night, my family would light the candles in a birch log.
Then we'd read a verse of the Christmas story from crumpled
strips of paper, tucked in the pockets of a felt Christmas tree
wall-hanging. We'd snap on the corresponding well-worn
ornament and end the devotional by singing.

On Sundays, my parents and their friends took turns hosting
Advent suppers and devotions. The vibe was boisterous and
warm. Lots of laughter, lots of soup, and always a time to gather
together for a reflection and singing.

So far, a COVID Advent looks promising. The Jacquie Lawson
Advent e-calendar is downloaded. We made wreaths this
afternoon on Zoom with a church group. Fifteen people
gathered for devotions online tonight.

There wasn't soup or hugs, but the same spirit of warmth and
caring was there. So were my parents, half a country away. Of
course we sang.

Oh come, oh come Emmanuel.

Sleep well world. God holds you.

November 30, 2020
Day 261

I'm teaching an Advent class on the beginning of Luke's gospel. It's called "People Who Waited" and it focuses on three poetic responses to news of Jesus' coming: Zechariah's Benedictus, Mary's Magnificat, and Simeon's Nunc Dimittis.

These are well-known in liturgical traditions. They have been sung and prayed for as long as people have been following Jesus.

As I dive into them, I sense the company of those who have trusted God in extraordinarily hard times. I imagine the music of earlier centuries, wafting into starry nights and chanted in monastic cells. I feel the hope and the blessing of prayers written thousands of years ago yet also written for today.

From the Benedictus:

> In the tender compassion of our God
> the dawn from on high shall break upon us,
> to shine on those who dwell in darkness and the
> shadow of death, and to guide our feet into the way of
> peace. (Luke 1:78–79)

Sleep well world. God holds you.

December 1, 2020
Day 262

Yesterday, I emailed my Christmas wish list to my family. Today, I made a different kind of wish list: my list of longings.

The Biblical texts I'm working with this week are all about longing in some form or fashion. People longed for a new government, for health, for children, for a close-knit community, for forgiveness, for peace with justice, for a future. They longed to be right with God.

During a community Bible Study, I asked participants to write down what they're longing for. COVID has created a deep well of longing. We did this exercise on Zoom, while listening to a five-hundred year old song of praise and blessing. It was holy.

I don't think I'll get most of the things on my Christmas wish list, and I don't think my longings will all be met over time.

Still, I believe there's great value in getting clear about what I want, getting clear about what Scripture shows us God wants, and seeing how those things come together. More importantly, I believe God can be counted on to work miracles that are so unexpected, they don't show up on a list.

Sleep well world. God holds you.

December 2, 2020
Day 263

I've had low energy since Thanksgiving. That's almost a week so it can't just be the sleep-inducing effects of a big turkey dinner. I think it's a combination of less sunlight, too much to do, a kid who wakes me up multiple times a night, and the existential stress of living through the coronavirus.

Psalm 85:6 says, "Will you not revive us again, Oh Lord, so that your people may rejoice in you?"

I love the word *revive*. It means "brought back to life." I notice the request is plural. It's not just me who needs reviving. It's a lot of people. It might be everybody. And it's not just individuals, but our communities, and the earth itself. God will rebuild it all with righteousness and truth and mercy and peace.

As much as I am eager to be a part of this future, I'm darn grateful for the reminder that God is the reviver, not me. God is the one who makes this all happen. So while I'm not exactly sitting these days out, I am going slow, saying "no," and trusting that God will bring me back to life in due time.

Sleep well world. God holds you.

December 3, 2020
Day 264

Advent is a time of waiting. It feels almost like punishment to enter a season set aside for waiting while, for the last nine months, we've done little else.

Recently, my waiting has taken on a decidedly domestic bent. It reminds me of another time: when I was expecting my children. Like many soon-to-be-parents, I developed a "nesting" instinct. I spent quiet hours folding baby clothes and cleaning out closets. I stayed close to home, full of patient, heavy expectation. My days always included walks, naps, hot water bottles, and tea.

Typically, my Advent is so full of concerts, shopping trips, and worship services that the waiting is an annoyance, not a spiritual practice. It's hard to wait when I'm rushing around.

This year is not typical. My usual flurry of activity is tempered by physical constraints of COVID, uncertainty about how to plan ahead, and a much lighter social schedule. I've noticed my nesting instinct is back as I clean out closets and deck my halls.

This waiting time will end. Something is being born. I know it has to do with Jesus. Beyond that I only perceive it faintly, in glimmer and flutter and dream and rhythm and silence. I trust it though. I trust God. New life is on its way.

Sleep well world. God holds you.

December 6, 2020
Day 267

"Rend your hearts and not your clothing." (Joel 2:13)

Today I preached to the broken-hearted people of God. I tried to follow the prophet Joel's lead and bless the sorrow that simply is part of living in a country laid low by a plague. Over 250,000 people have died. Food lines stretch long and days of isolation do too.

There's no shame in being sad about it. And we don't always need to cast blame. We can just feel it sometimes. Heartbroken.

I referenced the Hasidic teaching that God's word is written on our hearts so that when our hearts break, God can fall in.

Sleep well world. God holds you.

December 7, 2020
Day 268

Our worship team met tonight to finalize Christmas plans. As I was awed by their efforts, this question came to mind: *Why is every church working so hard to produce similar content?*

I don't mean that cynically. I ask it in order to understand if, given what's possible with technology, it's the most faithful use of our time.

One church could put together a Christmas Eve service, stream it to a million people, and call it a night. That's extreme. But such collaborations are certainly springing up, enabled by technology and fueled by exhaustion. For instance:

– I'm in a preaching rotation where once a month, pastors take turns preaching to four congregations.

– The Sunday after Christmas we're joining a different congregation's service on Zoom so our staff can have the day completely off; we'll return the favor the following Sunday.

– Our congregation will use a worship service produced for the whole denomination for Epiphany on January 6.

These collaborations are the exception. Mostly we are doing our own thing, working hard to keep our congregations fed, worshiping God with the people we have available, and using our voices, our stories, our talents, and our testimonies.

I don't have a great answer as to why we're still doing so much on our own. I need to keep thinking about this. Why do I like that most of our worship is homegrown and local? It's not because I preach the best sermons or because we couldn't find professional virtual choirs on YouTube to download instead of going through all the effort of getting our people synced up.

The words that keep coming to mind are *relationships* and *participation*. Church is about God and people. Worship is a key way these relationships are built. Worship isn't something you *watch*, it's something you *do*. Our church has great worship and it's not only because it's technically well-executed; it's because it's done by people who love and care for each other.

Sleep well world. God holds you.

December 8, 2020
Day 269

The story of God is a story of bodies. Mary's body changed when she said yes to God's call. The disciples followed Jesus not just with their thoughts and their feelings, but with their bodies too.

We await the incarnation of God. In Jesus, God has a body.

This year has been a lesson on the importance of bodies. Bodies have nasal passages and immune systems. Bodies have neural pathways that work better when they get a hug. Bodies need protection and care. They have skin and history. They need food and shelter and air to breathe. They can be the site of miracles. They can be the site of crimes.

Mary sang about her soul, saying that it "magnifies the Lord," (Luke 1:46) but it was her body that brought him into the world.

Sleep well world. God holds you.

December 9, 2020
Day 270

I used the *New York Times* calculator to find out where I am in the vaccine line. I'm behind 286.7 million people. That's only counting the United States. I'm really hopeful about the vaccine, but that's a lot of logistics between me and those shots.

That's not a complaint. I am healthy, under sixty, and I can do most of my work from home. I should be last.

It's a reminder, though, that we're going to still need each other to be responsible and show some restraint in the service of love. This isn't over with the snap of a finger. And there's still no vaccine for most of what ails us. I'm thinking of climate change and racism, for starters.

There's a pattern in the Psalms: God restores people from exile and sorrow back into community and health. Then they fall away again, so God does it again. Paraphrasing Psalm 126: remember that time God helped us? Uh, we need help again.

I'm a big believer in the vaccine. And I know we will still always need what vaccines can never give. May the love of God restore us. And then do it again.

Sleep well world. God holds you.

December 10, 2020
Day 271

In the early days of the pandemic, our kids often made plans for "after the sickness." We had long mental lists of all the waterparks and shows and museums we'd go to, after. I recently noticed that somewhere along the line, they stopped talking that way. They pretty much live contentedly within the limits of the coronavirus.

In Psalm 126, people who weep also sow seeds. Their present planting results in future joy.

I've noticed myself thinking more and more about "after." I am fixed on a few dates like they are lights in a distant harbor. Easter. Memorial Day. The start of school. They are just beginning to come into sight, if not into focus.

Even though we're in some of the worst days of the virus, it's time to reintroduce the concept of "after the sickness" to the kids.

I'm glad they're content, but I also want them to look forward to birthday parties, boisterous playgrounds, and big family sing-alongs. Church. School. Seeing people's real smiles. Today we talked about how magical it will be to see *The Nutcracker* live, someday.

I don't want to get their hopes up only to be dashed; that would be cruel. But I notice I have started dreaming again. Now is the time to plant seeds for the joy that is coming.

Sleep well world. God holds you.

December 13, 2020
Day 274

Today was our church's annual Advent Carol Festival. I participated by Zooming from home with a wiggly daughter on my lap. It was marvelous to see people I love share their musical gifts. Violin. Piano. Voice. Bells.

By the end, our whole family was belting out hymns. I swear I could tell, from the smile on one musician's face, that he delighted in watching all the Zoomers sing along at home through multiple modulations of "Joy to the World." It truly was a communal experience, even though we could only hear him and his harpsichord.

Singing to a screen is not the same as singing in person. But, as I'm fond of saying these days, it's not nothing. I felt like I sang with more than just my family today. I sang with my church.

I am simply grateful for all the ways musicians are creating ways for us to make music together. Let heaven and nature sing indeed.

Sleep well world. God holds you.

December 14, 2020
Day 275

Today, the first vaccine was administered in the United States. Our COVID death toll passed 300,000. Joe Biden and Kamala Harris were affirmed by the Electoral College. It was a big day in the news.

Meanwhile in my tiny corner of the kingdom, I visited three of our most stalwart members in the senior center where they live. It was the first time I'd seen them since March. We all took precautions and sat in a big lobby, distanced and masked.

They are some of the oldest and long-term members of our church. One, German by birth, lived through the ravages of World War II as a girl. The others, a couple who had an interracial marriage before it was legal, have over one hundred years of government service between them.

They have all lived through some stuff. And now they are living through this.

Jesus ministered against a backdrop of political power struggles, sickness, religious in-fighting, and economic disparity. He focused on individual people and small communities who were trying to live faithfully. The gospels are full of the stories of the people he encountered on roadsides, dinner tables, and little synagogues along the way.

It was good to visit my people. I held up my phone and showed photos of my kids. I played a clip of our virtual choir on our church's YouTube page. They were delighted. The music made us cry.

They expressed their worries about the country and their hopes that things will improve. We recorded a greeting to share with the rest of the church. We prayed.

I left poinsettias as a sign of the hope of Christmas and a tangible reminder of the love we share..

Sleep well world. God holds you.

December 15, 2020
Day 276

I'm typically a confident person, but during COVID I've noticed more self-doubt creeping in.

I think it has to do with the limits of online feedback in moments of vulnerability. Preaching into the void of a screen is like baring your soul to someone who responds with a snore. It's often demoralizing.

I appreciate chat sidebars, Facebook likes, and emojis. I really do. But they aren't the same as the hush that falls over an attentive congregation or the shifting in a seat that lets me know I hit a nerve.

During the pandemic, I've taught classes where half the students had their cameras off. I send emails that never get answered. I sometimes want to yell into my computer, *Is anybody out there?*

At the same time, I have been woefully unresponsive to others. Texts and emails go unanswered, sometimes forever. I multitask my way through too many meetings, only half-attentive with my own camera turned off too.

Today I noticed the embodied response Elizabeth, great-with-child, gave her young niece Mary. Newly pregnant, Mary was full of faith in God but also probably full of fear and insecurity.

Elizabeth greeted Mary warmly, saying, "As soon as I heard your voice, the baby in my womb leapt for joy." (Luke 1:44)

What a perfect welcome for a vulnerable person.

In moments when my confidence craters, I'm going to try to remember that it's not just me. Something is missing.

I'm going to try to bring to mind the fullness of Elizabeth's response. Hear it as my own. And respond to others as fully as I can, until we meet again.

Sleep well world. God holds you.

December 16, 2020
Day 277

COVID got real again today. The death toll du jour includes two names of people I know, albeit remotely. One was an acquaintance in college. The other is my sister-in-law's good friend's dad. I know about their deaths only because I know people who care about them. Still, I was moved. Their deaths tapped into the vein of grief that's right under the surface.

I don't think I'm drawing on a grief that isn't mine. I do wonder, though, why it takes someone whose name I know to die to remind me that this thing is close, real, and devastating. Like most people, I tend not to understand what's happening to other people until I have a personal connection.

The vaccination got real today too. I was in a FaceTime conversation with the first person I actually know to get vaccinated. I rejoiced at her visible relief. The promise of the vaccine stanched my grief.

Maybe this is why we need Christmas. God got real for us so we would know grace and love, justice and peace. God knew we couldn't just hear about it; we had to experience it. God made flesh. Love up close.

I pray tonight for all the people for whom COVID is too real, especially for the families of the two who I know who died today.

Sleep well world. God holds you.

December 17, 2020
Day 278

During the pandemic, Bible study has become even more important to me. I almost always say some version of the same prayer at the start of group Bible studies. I've developed it over time, settling into it. This is the first time I've actually written it down.

I realized the other day that I borrowed the image of Christ taking "lodging in our hearts" from my favorite Advent song, "The Dream Isaiah Saw," lyrics by Thomas Troeger.[17] I hope he won't mind. Here's the prayer:

> Holy God, as we encounter your living word with this group of people, speak the word we need to hear. Give us a word of comfort and a word of challenge. Kindle our faith.
>
> Open our ears.
> Open our minds.
> Open our hearts, that you take lodging there.

Sleep well world. God holds you.

December 20, 2020
Day 281

A baby's due date is calculated as nine months from conception. That's two-hundred and eighty days. We've been in the pandemic long enough to have a baby.

Churches celebrate the annunciation—when the Angel Gabriel told Mary about her pregnancy—on March 25, nine months before Christmas. It didn't occur to me to take note of that, back on Day 11. It didn't occur to me that we'd be in COVID long enough for Jesus to be born.

I'm looking ahead nine months more. September. I sense that God is announcing things now about how holy the future could be. Patience. Be not afraid. Nine months out. What beauty is starting now? What miracle is on its way?

Sleep well world. God holds you.

December 21, 2020
Day 282

Solstice.

The date for Christmas was set as December 25 because it's the first day after the winter solstice that a person can perceive that the days are getting longer. I look forward to longer days and to Christmas, but first I want to soak in the sacred length of this night.

Many churches hold "blue Christmas services" tonight. We did one last year but in the name of simplicity, we cut it out of our repertoire this year.

Last year, we read from Barbara Brown Taylor's *Learning to Walk in the Dark*. She teaches people to trust darkness and befriend it. The night—literal and spiritual—is a time in which you can discover great intimacy with God.[18]

This has been true during the pandemic. It's not just that light shines in the darkness, it's that the darkness itself is holy, generative, and healing.

An evening prayer:

> O God, you have called your servants to ventures of which we cannot see the ending, by paths as yet untrodden, through perils unknown. Give us faith to go out with good courage, not knowing where we go, but only that your hand is leading us and your love supporting us; through Jesus Christ our Lord. Amen.[19]

Sleep well world. God holds you.

December 22, 2020
Day 283

I went out the last two nights to catch a glimpse of the convergence of the planets, but alas, I didn't see it. I didn't really even know where to look.

Beyond the fact that it's a cool, rare event, this convergence has taken on a bigger meaning. All manner of people are out looking for it, all around the world. It's like it's a sign.

A Christmas star. A brightness in the heavens. Christians are conditioned to hear of such things and think of Jesus' birth. This year, I notice even people who normally aren't wired for faith are yearning for indications of God's presence. Who doesn't want to hear that the future will be OK? That the power of love is still the strongest thing? That the mystery of God has been revealed?

The angel told the shepherds, "This will be a sign for you. You will find a child wrapped in bands of cloths and lying in a manger." (Luke 2:12)

I don't normally throw in with the "signs reading" crowd, but I'll go back out tomorrow and look up at the sky. I think it's the last day the convergence of the planets will be visible.

If I don't see it though, I'll count my own lucky stars that everywhere I look these days, the signs are clear. God is with us.

Sleep well world. God holds you.

December 23, 2020
Day 284

If ever there was a time to go to church, tomorrow
night—Christmas Eve, 2020—is it.

The internet is going to be a festival of soaring angel song,
extraordinary preaching, and candles lit at exactly the right
moment to evoke a peace that would lull a babe to sleep,

Pastors and church musicians have spent all their creative
effort on tomorrow night, when we deliver the news of
God-made-flesh in a decidedly unfleshy way: through camera
and radio signal and digital code. Especially this year, we
desperately want our people to know the joy, peace, and love
of Jesus. Especially this year, we're not sure how it will go.

It will work. The good news will reach living rooms and
nursing homes and hospital beds and maybe even a few
shepherds keeping watch in their fields, pulling out their
phones to join the worship.

It's going to be amazing.

At some point tomorrow, all the services will be over. It will
be out of our hands. I always imagine on Christmas Eve, after
everyone has gone to sleep, there's a hitch of a
moment—Madeleine L'Engle might call it a wrinkle in
time[20]—in which God does something small and powerful and
unstoppable. And it doesn't depend on us at all.

Sleep well world. God holds you.

SECTION 4

THREE WEEKS OF REVELATION
January 3, 2021 – January 21, 2021

"In the time of King Herod, after Jesus was born in
Bethlehem of Judea, wise men from the East came to
Jerusalem, asking, 'Where is the child who has been born king
of the Jews? For we observed his star at its rising, and have
come to pay him homage.' When King Herod heard this, he
was frightened, and all Jerusalem with him." (Matthew 2:1–3)

~~~

"History will rightly remember today's violence at the Capitol,
incited by a sitting president who has continued to baselessly
lie about the outcome of a lawful election, as a moment of
great dishonor and shame for our nation."
  —*Former U.S. President Barack Obama, January 6, 2021*[1]

"Resolved, That Donald John Trump, President of the United
States, is impeached for high crimes and mis-demeanors."
  —*Articles of Impeachment, January 13, 2021* [2]

"There is always light, if only we're brave enough to see it.
If only we're brave enough to be it."
  —*Amanda Gorman, "The Hill We Climb," Inaugural Poem
  for the Inauguration of Joseph R. Biden, January 20, 2021*[3]

.

January 3, 2021
Day 295

I took some time off after Christmas. A quick getaway. The New Year. And now I'm back at it.

I preached this morning about the time that the boy Jesus, aged twelve, hung out in the temple for three days while his parents searched frantically. (Luke 2:41–51)

I keyed in on the disconnect between the "great anxiety" that Mary expressed and the calm that Jesus exuded.

This is where much of my Christian life is played out, in that landscape between my great worries and God's great peace.

There is plenty of cause for anxiety right now, as COVID-19 mutates, the viral mixing bowl of holiday travel incubates, and the president tries to steal the election.

There's plenty of cause for calm too, and I don't just mean that the vaccine and cooler political heads will prevail.

I mean Jesus. True peace comes from trusting that in Christ, God has already redeemed the world and everything in it. Believing that, I have no reason to be anxious.

Still, it rarely works to simply tell myself, *God's got this,* when worry gets the best of me. I need people, food, song, story, symbol, proof.

I noted that Jesus didn't say to his mom, "Will you just chill and trust me?"

Instead, he left the temple and went back home. He traversed the landscape of her anxiety and brought her his peace.

Sleep well world. God holds you.

January 4, 2021
Day 296

"You are my son, my beloved." (Luke 3:22)

Today as my kindergartner logged into school after winter break, I had a twinge of sadness to think she might return to in-person class as soon as next week. I don't think it's going to happen then. I hope for everyone's health it doesn't. But it will happen someday. I want it to happen someday.

A definite silver lining of the pandemic has been the closeness I've gotten with my kids. Yes, sometimes the challenge of multitasking around their constant presence makes me want to beg, *Can't you please just leave me alone?* But some days the time with the kids is pure magic.

As we inch toward the light at the end of the COVID tunnel, I'm starting to think about how I want life to be different.

I want to cherish my kids and make sure that I don't slip back into pre-pandemic patterns, when too many days the only times I saw them were the hours engaged in a struggle to get to daycare or to bed. I want to have more unstressed time with my beloved kids, for my sake and for theirs.

Sleep well world. God holds you.

January 5, 2021
Day 297

I've been silent on the political turmoil of recent weeks because I think it's mostly bluster and distraction, the beast thrashing wildly while falling to its demise. I want to focus on Jesus and the hope, light, and joy all around. But the story of Jesus is also the story of the beast.

A thrashing beast can do serious damage. Evil never gets mortally wounded, it just skulks away to regroup. White supremacists gather in the capital. COVID numbers are out of control.

Tomorrow is the Epiphany, when we celebrate the Wise Men's visit to pay homage to the toddler king Jesus. It's a story of cosmic chosenness and the joy of true worship. It's a story that expands the purpose of Jesus beyond a small group out to the whole world. It's wonderful. Revelation and generosity and wisdom.

It's also about an insecure, threatened king who lies and plots to destroy his competition. Herod orders the Wise Men to reveal Jesus' whereabouts. They disobey and go home by another way. On the heels of the Epiphany comes the slaughter of the innocents. King Herod, in an attempt to murder Jesus, kills all the little boys. Jesus escapes this time, becoming a refugee in Egypt. But oh, the collateral damage is heart-wrenching.

"A voice is heard in Ramah, weeping and great mourning, Rachel weeping for her children and refusing to be comforted, because they are no more." (Matt 2:18)

Sleep well world. God holds you.

January 6, 2021
Day 298

Day of Epiphany.

As my post, I am copying the pastoral email I wrote this evening to the congregation I serve.

Dear Church,

I'm sending this special note tonight in response to the breach at the Capitol today. It was unsettling, enraging, and profoundly disturbing. If you found yourself in disbelief, horror, tears, and dismay, please know you were not alone. I was right there with you in spirit, as one who loves the people of this country and believes part of our Christian calling is to work for our country's well-being.

I don't think, however, the attempted coup was all that surprising. The violence, white supremacy, and disdain for national institutions that we saw today has long been the rhetoric of our country's highest leader and has been simmering for a long time.

Today is also the day of Epiphany, when the Wise Men followed the star to Jesus. They worshiped him with the true joy that comes from an encounter with our living God. Their worship had consequences. By honoring Jesus as their king, they demonstrated that their true loyalty belonged to God, not to the cruel and jealous Herod.

We follow Jesus. In him, God was born to this world to show us the way of love, joy, peace, and humility. That way saves us from the violence and hatred we all carry. Jesus saves us. Jesus also leads us to oppose the disdain for justice and carelessness for human lives that we saw today.

Tonight, I am praying. I encourage you to pray too. I also encourage you to:

— Hold fast to Jesus and the peace he gives.

— Not to turn from your neighbor in hatred and not to discount anyone as beyond redemption, but to pursue love.

— Continue to work for the well-being of all the people of this land, which also means to care especially for those who have been marginalized in our national pursuit of justice. Black Lives Matter.

— Finally, go very, very gentle on yourselves. This has been a disturbing day in the midst of a disturbing time. It is unrealistic to expect that you can simply go on with life as normal.

Be at Peace, Pastor Sarah

Sleep well world. God holds you.

January 7, 2021
Day 299

In the last day and a half, I have consumed too many words. Descriptions. Laments. Analysis. Speeches. Editorials. Texts. Diagnoses. Trainings. Conversations. Prayers.

It's good to stay informed and learn as much as possible. But it's become counterproductive and threatens to drown out God's voice.

Listen.

God's word moved over the waters, creating order out of formless chaos: "Let there be light." (Gen 1:3)

God's word resounded in Jesus' ear: "You are my beloved, with you I am well pleased." (Luke 3:22)

Those are the words I want to spend time with. That's the voice I need to hear.

Sleep well world. God holds you.

January 10, 2021
Day 302

Do not be afraid.

As I scan my feelings about the past days, chief among them is fear. I fear for our national security, our children's futures, people who are targets of hatred, my own soul.

In the New Testament, the words "do not be afraid" show up something like seventy times. (Don't quote me on the number. I'm too tired to count.)

Believing that God is serious about this "fear not" business, I ask myself, *How should I live so that others are not afraid?* Wear a mask, stay away from crowds, etc. I prioritize safety and hope others do the same for me.

The problem is that humans aren't very good at keeping one another safe. We're all too damaged, the pleasures of risky behavior too alluring, and the unknowns of life too complex.

The words "do not be afraid" are usually followed by "for the Lord your God . . ."

I'm trying to remember that my security doesn't rest in my national identity, my proximity to the Pentagon, the ease with which I can avoid the coronavirus, or even my circle of support.

My security rests in God. And that's not because God gives me safety, but because God gives me love.

I am praying through my fears tonight. Trying to welcome them, name them and give them to God. I may not feel safe, but I do know that I am profoundly loved, and perfect love—God's love—casts out fear. (1 John 4:18)

Sleep well world. God holds you.

January 11, 2021
Day 303

Last night, at the end of an emotionally raw day, my daughters, ages five and four, decided to "salon" me. They mashed up avocado with honey and lemon, and smeared it on my face. They pressed sliced cucumbers into my eye sockets. Their little hands massaged gobs of lotion into mine.

They took care of me.

I have been focusing on pastoral care-giving more than ever before. My instinct to give care has a decidedly physical aspect. I wish I could wrap everyone in prayer shawls, brew cups of tea, and cook good, warm food.

I can't always find the words to untangle the moral universe, but I can bake a lasagna. And that might do as much to convey Christ's presence as any perfectly wrought sermon.

At some point during the coronavirus, our younger daughter took to saying, "I love you and I care about you." I don't know where she got that, but it melts my heart every time. I know it's true. I've got avocado goop in my hair to prove it.

Sleep well world. God holds you.

January 12, 2021
Day 304

I don't have any words tonight so I'm posting this prayer. It was sent to us on a handwritten card by our children's minister. It hangs on our daughter's bulletin board in at-home kindergarten. We say it most mornings right before she logs onto school.

> Dear God. Now that I start my day,
> I offer you my heart and pray.
> Guide me in everything I do and
> keep me always close to you. Amen.

Sleep well world. God holds you.

January 13, 2021
Day 305

A week after a rebel mob broke into the Capitol, Congress impeached the president for a second time, this time for inciting an insurrection.

That is a surreal sentence, and it doesn't even mention that we're in a pandemic.

With all this, I sighed with relief when I realized the psalm for the week was my favorite. Psalm 139. I was introduced to this Psalm when a family friend paraphrased it on the jacket of a prayer book she gave me when I was headed to the Peace Corps. I still have that book in a box of memorabilia. With its assurance of God's presence through time and space, Psalm 139 has been a touchstone ever since.

I've read this Psalm hundreds of times. But apparently I only digested the beginning. I never noticed that the end is about conflict. It mentions rebellion, "I abhor those who rebel against you," and it assumes enemies, asking God to "slay the wicked." (Ps 139)

Scripture always sounds different depending on the context. It's what makes it so alive. In the midst of the surreal news of the week, I heard a very familiar word of God very differently.

At the end, the psalmist conveys hope that in a time of tumult, he would withstand the test: "See that there is no offensive way in me, and lead me in the way everlasting." (Ps 139:24) That prayer too, is mine.

Sleep well world. God holds you.

January 14, 2021
Day 306

On Thursdays I always email a note to the congregation I serve. This was part of what I sent today:

> *Last week during worship, I cried. Many of you noticed and reached out. You asked "are you OK?" to which the answer is "yes and no." I am OK in that I am healthy, my family is well, and I trust Jesus. But I am not OK in ways that maybe you share: I am disoriented, grief-stricken, pierced by all this hatred, and soul-searching.*

These days are fraught. As often happens, worship was when my floodgates opened.

In worship, with the community of church, God is present to me in a way that I don't experience at other times. Especially during communion, the Spirit reminds me that "broken and blessed" is a pattern of the Christian life.

I am grateful for a God and a community that I can trust enough to be a whole, real person. And I am grateful that as always happens, tears gave way to singing in the end.

Sleep well world. God holds you.

January 17, 2021
Day 309

Coronavirus cases rise, vaccinations are ramping up, and yet that seems like below-the-fold news compared to the upcoming inauguration.

I'm remembering the events surrounding Barack Obama's first inauguration. The day preceding it was Martin Luther King Jr. Day, and it was declared a National Day of Service

A huge, free concert on the National Mall with a star-studded line-up happened that week. There were also scores of lectures, art shows, and films. The mood was so jubilant. So free.

I remember hearing Bettye LaVette and Jon Bon Jovi cover Sam Cooke's "A Change Is Gonna Come." It was a heady weekend. It felt like a page of American history was turning. The future seemed so bright.

Yesterday, I biked around the National Mall. It's blocked off, but in the soft perimeter, observers are allowed. I wanted to see the scene for myself. I've never seen security so tight. It is crawling with military personnel and looks like a war zone. It will be a very different inauguration than others, but the task will get done. The evil that the current administration has come to represent won't just go away, but I am hopeful for a new day.

"It's been a long time coming but I know, a change is gonna come."[4]

Sleep well world. God holds you.

January 18, 2021
Day 310

Martin Luther King Jr. Day.

Our church was led in a conversation on racial trauma and anxiety tonight. The facilitator invited us to pay attention to our physical responses to images of racialized trauma. Breath. Fists. Backs. Tears. Emotions lodge in bodies. Trauma is passed down in flesh, through generations.

In a year when most of my human interactions have been with disembodied heads on computer screens, never have I thought so much about bodies.

A few years back, the Rev. William Barber revived The Poor People's campaign, which MLK was working on when he was murdered. Today, the *New York Times* quoted Barber as saying: "We must now go about the business of lifting up those who are poor and those without health care. That's the only way we can heal the nation. We have to heal the body."[5]

"You are all the body of Christ, and individually members of it," wrote the apostle Paul. (1 Cor 12:27) I don't just think he was talking metaphorically. We have to heal the body.

Sleep well world. God holds you.

January 19, 2021
Day 311

Tonight's memorial at the reflecting pool was the first time our nation has been called to grieve together for the over 400,000 dead from the coronavirus in our country. It was brief, powerful and overdue.

Houses of worship across the country rang bells as a memorial. Our church rang our bell too.

On one side of me in the belfry was a church member whose brother, also a member, died from the virus. On the other side were my young daughters, their little faces captivated with every peal.

I pulled on that heavy rope forty times, standing in the place between death and life, grief and hope.

Since then, Bob Dylan's song, "Ring Them Bells" has been in my head.

"Ring them bells sweet Martha for the poor man's son. Ring them bells so the world will know that our God is one."[6]

It's my prayer tonight.*

Sleep well world. God holds you.

In the original post, I included a link to the song.

January 20, 2021
Day 312

Inauguration.

Neck deep in the chaos of last summer, a leader in our denomination told me he was keeping his eye on artists. He predicted that they'd give us the language, images, and melodies we need to envision a new future.

Today's inauguration was a bonanza of great art. Song, dance, flags, lights, fashion, fireworks, film, and poetry—oh the poetry. I laughed and cried and danced and was flat-out stunned by what humans can do.

Vincent Van Gogh conceived of Jesus "as an artist greater than all other artists . . . working in the living flesh."[7]

As I join so many others in hoping that today our country begins a new chapter, I love this concept of the artist Jesus, making something new and beautiful of us all.

Sleep well world. God holds you.

January 21, 2021
Day 313

I've heard the term "inflection point" a lot lately. It's a calculus term and means the point where a curve changes direction.

On Sunday, our church will hear about one of the disciple Peter's inflection points, when he first followed Jesus. In one of the Gospels, this event is recorded with almost robotic automation. Jesus saw Peter and his fishing buddies, told them to leave everything to follow him, and they did.

In another version, though, there's a lot more context. Peter responded to Jesus' call only after Jesus performed miracles that were quite personal for Peter—healing his mother-in-law and filling his nets with fish. Peter had also heard him preach, and importantly, told Jesus the truth about his own sinfulness. (Luke 5)

I hope our society is about to change direction. I think it will be driven by many, many individual inflection points that are the result of sustained relationships, much more like the second version of Peter's call. God appears in tangible love and healing miracle, through policies and people, to bring the abundance and forgiveness that allows people to trust Jesus.

I think this is the work of the church right now: to embody the love of God revealed in Jesus, so that people can change direction and follow his way with all we've got.

Sleep well world. God holds you.

SECTION 5

THE LAST DAYS OF A LONG LENT
January 25, 2021 – March 28, 2021

"For there is still a vision for the appointed time; it speaks of the end, and does not lie. If it seems to tarry, wait for it; it will surely come, it will not delay." (Habakkuk 2:3)

~ ~ ~

"A nation numbed by misery and loss is confronting a number that still has the power to shock: 500,000. . . . No other country has counted so many deaths in the pandemic. More Americans have perished from Covid-19 than on the battlefields of World War I, World War II and the Vietnam War combined."
  —*Julie Bosman, correspondent for the* New York Times, *February 21, 2021*[1]

"I think if somebody says I am now fully vaccinated, I want to go back to my church in person . . . I want to travel and visit my grandchildren. . . . We have sufficient evidence saying the vaccines protect you. They also will reduce the risk of your being an asymptomatic carrier. Please go out and do these things. Get your life back."
  —*Dr. Leana Wen, public health professor at George Washington University,* Washington Post, *March 14, 2021*[2]

January 25, 2021
Day 317

I want my shot! Technically, as a clergy person I qualify for the vaccine, but the backlog of requests plus limited quantity of doses mean I won't get it anytime soon. Nor should I. Other people really do need it more.

Why is it when something is close in view it is harder to wait?

I find myself almost forgetting about the virus—as if we are already vaccinated—even while these new variants sail around the globe and it's getting worse, not better. Today, as we were eating, I said to my husband, "That's it. Let's call a babysitter right now to watch the kids while we go to dinner." He pointed out that we were actually eating a fine dinner. And there's still a pandemic.

I think about the phrase "we're in this together" and recent calls for unity. I worry that a difficult phase of the pandemic is about to begin. When some are vaccinated and others are not, we will no longer be in this together, if we ever really were.

Jesus often left crowds of people clamoring for healing. It's one of the more astonishing details of his ministry. He healed some, but not all. I wonder if the others ever felt jealous. Jesus must have thought we would learn from his example, and the community would keep on healing people in his name.

I tell myself to have patience and keep choosing the things that will bring life. And I hope that when I cross into the community of the vaccinated, I will not forget what it was like to be on the other side.

Sleep well world. God holds you.

January 26, 2021
Day 318

I sense I'm entering a period of significant discernment. This is not some way of hinting at big plans. I have none, except to renovate the kitchen.

But within this life, this call, I am positive there are major changes afoot. It's mostly related to emerging from the pandemic shutdowns. Some of the ruts of the old life are so worn away that I can make new tracks. It's also related to my kids getting more independent and some normal shifts in the life of a church (staffing, capital campaign, mission, etc.)

I'm not sure when, but sometime soon a world of new possibilities will open up. It's terrifying and exhilarating.

I know that a time of change is a time for me to be committed to prayer. I also know that I am prayed for by other people.

Before Jesus called his disciples and changed their lives, he prayed all night long.

Jesus is praying too. What an amazing thought. Jesus is praying too. And the Holy Spirit intercedes with sighs too deep for words.

Sleep well world. God holds you.

January 27, 2021
Day 319

It's National Chocolate Cake Day!

I was informed of this by my exuberant kindergartner this morning right before she asked, "Mom, can we bake a cake?!"

I often overhear the first minutes of online kindergarten. Her teachers always note the significance of the day. "Hat Day." "Rubber Ducky Day." Yesterday was "National Plan Your Vacation Day." Really.

Today is also the feast day of Saint Lydia, for whom our younger daughter is named. Lydia was known for her hospitality. She welcomed the apostle Paul into her home.

Tonight I'm getting together with two of my best friends from college. We typically take turns hosting each other every year. This time it's virtual, of course. In a pandemic version of hospitality, one of them sent tea bags in the mail so we could all sip our brew together online.

Hospitality runs deeper than cake or tea or even welcoming someone into your home.

Christian hospitality is grounded in the idea that with any person you welcome, you also welcome Christ. The person who needs hospitality is not a burden but a gift. It's a mutual exchange, often not clear who is the guest and who is the host.

"Welcome one another as Christ has welcomed you." (Rom 15:17)

COVID-19 has changed the mechanisms of hospitality, but not its necessity. It's there in every well-orchestrated Zoom meeting, every phone call where true listening occurs, and every online classroom where teachers make space for all sorts of silliness.

The cake is done. The house smells sweet. The water is boiling for tea, and the Zoom will start soon.

Sleep well world. God holds you.

January 28, 2021
Day 320

My parents got their vaccines!

I remember that when the coronavirus was first spreading in the U.S., my parents went shopping. My dad hit up Barnes and Noble and the bird food store. My mom went to buy fabric. It was like they were getting supplies to last them through a bad storm. I was emotional and excessively concerned they had just gotten sick. Those were the early days. My parents soon stopped going out at all. Poor birds. I think they've gone hungry ever since.

The vaccine doesn't change my parents' immediate horizon. They will keep a tight circle until more people are vaccinated. It does change a lot though, chiefly that we all no longer have the ever-present worry the virus could be fatal for them. What a relief. They are going to make it.

My kids asked, "Can they come visit?" Soon kiddos. Soon.

The psalmist says, "I will praise the Lord with my whole heart." (Ps 111:1) I know what that feels like, tonight.

Sleep well world. God holds you.

February 1, 2021
Day 324

Pre-COVID, today would have been a snow day. As it was, virtual school technically carried on but our girls pretty much took the day off anyway. I did too. I needed a break.

A New Jersey township declared that even during the era of online learning, they'd still have snow days. They wrote, "We will maintain the hope of children by calling actual snow days during COVID."[3]

They got it right. I've come to think of taking a sabbath as a planned snow day, with the joy, magic, rest, and play that can unspool at its own pace.

Today, I walked, rested, and read. I maintained my hope. I spent time with the God who restored a useless hand; who instructed people to be defined by rest, not work; and who told religious leaders yearning to prove their righteousness, "just stop." (Or something like that).

Turns out a snow day was exactly what I needed.

Sleep well world. God holds you.

February 2, 2021
Day 325

Groundhog Day.

In the movie *Groundhog Day*, the main character lives the same day over and over again. It's an apt description of coronatime, even though today is the first actual Groundhog Day of the pandemic.

A week ago I read a line in a novel, *Angle of Repose,* by Wallace Stegner, that resonated with a *Groundhog Day* existence:

> Imprisoned in reiterative seasons, vacillating between hope and disappointment, they were kept from being the vigorous doers that their nature and their culture instructed them to be. Their waiting blurred the calendar.[4]

"Their waiting blurred the calendar." I love that description. It's not boredom but blurriness. Flatness. Nothing sharp or distinct to look forward to.

"Kept from being a vigorous doers." Many days I have felt this intensely, trapped inside, at a computer, with little energy for anything extra. But not today. Today, on Groundhog Day of all days, I kept thinking, "Something is about to happen."

I went cross-country skiing, and faced with an open field of fresh snow, I was almost twitching with perception of the new thing that God is doing. I stood silently in prayer, and for the first time in a long time, I sensed not the blurriness of time, but its fullness.

Sleep well world. God holds you.

February 3, 2021
Day 326

Today we studied Psalm 147, which includes the words "God provides."

For countless households, COVID has sparked an economic crisis. Congress is currently debating a third stimulus package to help keep people out of poverty.

Meanwhile, the church I serve just passed its boldest budget in years. We don't know what the national economy will do, but we hear the call of God to our church, saying, "Keep going, I will provide."

We have good news to proclaim in word and deed. It is urgent and life-saving. In our new budget, we are maintaining our focus on worship and families. We added money for digital evangelism, racial justice, advocacy, and outreach. We cut our electrical bill because we're going solar, but that savings will not be enough to fund these other priorities.

I don't know what Congress will do, but the church I serve is going all-out to make the love of Jesus known this year.

Am I a little bit afraid we're not going to make it? Yes and no. Yes, because in church life we have no guarantees. At any point, people could just all stop giving, and it could all fall apart.

But no. I'm not really afraid. I know the people I serve and I trust God. As we give what we can, God will provide.

Sleep well world. God holds you.

February 4, 2021
Day 327

I burned palms today in preparation for Ash Wednesday. I remember when they arrived in time for Palm Sunday, ten long months ago. Back then, I arranged them artistically in the sanctuary for a worship service that only had a handful of in-person leaders. The rest of the church was online.

I remember boxing the palms up afterward and putting them in a corner to dry. I remember sensing that even a few people in the sanctuary was too risky. I remember knowing we wouldn't be back together there for a long time.

Today I found the palms right where I'd left them. I took them outside and set a foil-lined roasting pan in the snow. I broke desiccated palms into it. I put a lighter to the pile of palm pieces and for a few seconds, the flame was huge and burned clear. Then it simmered and the pan was ash and red snakes of cinder. I fed it more palms. This time it was mostly smoke. Great big billows. Within five minutes, all had burned, save one. I kept one palm branch out as a reminder of something. I'm not sure what.

I folded the ashes in the foil and drove them home. I will package them in tiny envelopes and distribute them to worshipers in time for Ash Wednesday.

This gathering, burning, and dusting made me feel like an ancient priest. Solitary. Tending a holy fire. Redolent air. Ashes escaping the bowl, circling high and landing on the snow. I thought about the people who have died. I thought of those yearning to be more alive.

Hours later, smoke lingers in my hair. I'd be unrecognizable as an ancient priest, with my femaleness and children and chaotic suburban home. But their work is my work too. Burning palms. Tending ashes. Participating in mystery. Preparing people for death and then for the life to come.

"Let my prayer rise before you as incense, the lifting up of my hands as the evening sacrifice." (Ps 141:2)

Sleep well world. God holds you.

February 8, 2021
Day 331

Super Bowl Sunday.

Last year for the Super Bowl, we crammed multiple couches into our little living room and hosted some friends. It was the last time we entertained inside our home (and relatedly, the last time our whole house was clean).

We're coming up on the year-long anniversary of the pandemic, and I'm aware of all the "lasts before COVID." Last meal out. Last vacation.

We had no idea. It's shocking to remember how quickly things changed.

I suppose we often don't know something will be the last until it is too late to appreciate it. The disciples certainly didn't understand that their special Passover dinner with Jesus was the Last Supper.

In that meal, Jesus gave them a ritual of love that would get them through the awful days ahead. They were able to cling to the memory of Jesus' presence, until they met him again for the first time.[5]

I don't know when we'll be able to host a crowd of people indoors again, but I hope it is soon. I sure am glad for the memories and for the promise of the days to come.

Sleep well world. God holds you.

February 9, 2021
Day 332

I can't get myself to finish upcoming worship plans. This
Sunday, Transfiguration, we're supposed to symbolically bury
the Alleluias. Wednesday we will be marked with crosses of ash
on our foreheads: "Remember you are dust and to dust you
shall return." (Gen 3:19)

Lent is a week away. Last year, congregants were making
intentional commitments to pray and fast during Lent. By
week three, most of us scrapped our plans in order to attend
to very present concerns for mortality and scarcity. We didn't
need the practice of Lent; we were living it.

It's been a long Lent. I'm tempted to say we don't need Ash
Wednesday this year. It seems cruel to ask people to give
something up; misguided to think that people need reminding
that suffering and repentance are part of the journey with
Jesus.

Some congregants have already told me, "I just don't want to
do it this year." I get it.

Even so, I will lead us back into Lent, trusting that there's
something to be found there. We will do the rituals even if
we're not in the mood.

Lent will end. It will. It doesn't end in death; it ends in life.
Our preparations aren't for sorrow; they're for glory. I will go
through Lent this year, but my eyes won't be fixed on the cross,
as in years past. Instead, they will be fixed on the empty tomb.

Sleep well world. God holds you.

February 11, 2021
Day 334

Psalm day. You can't make this stuff up.

Against the backdrop of the former President's impeachment
trial for inciting insurrection, we were served up Psalm 36 today.
It has lines like:

"He has smooth-talked himself into believing that his evil will
never be noticed," (Ps 36:2, MSG) and "He plays with fire and
doesn't care who gets burned." (Ps 36:4, MSG)

The Psalms often place people in overly simple categories, eg:
wicked or righteous, enemy or friend. I do that too. The Psalms
often beg for vengeance. I do that too. I know it's not good
when I do these things, but how are we to understand it in the
Psalms?

A sidebar in my Bible explains it well. "These are prayers of
people who have been severely mistreated . . . the point isn't
personal payback but rather a deep desire that God set things
right for those whose lives are threatened."[6]

"A deep desire that God set things right." Indeed.

The impeachment trial may or may not bring some justice. Most
other injustices from this past year will go unexamined. It is
distressing to consider, unless I weigh it against something
Psalm 36 points out: the scale on which the wicked operate is
minuscule compared to the extent of God's love and justice.

> God's love is meteoric,
> his loyalty astronomic,
> His purpose titanic,

his verdicts oceanic.
Yet in his largeness
nothing gets lost;
Not a man, not a mouse,
slips through the cracks. (Ps 36:5-6, MSG)

Sleep well world. God holds you.

February 12, 2021
Day 335

At our church council meeting tonight, nearly everyone expressed that they feel behind. I heard "disorganized," "overwhelmed," and "the to-do list isn't getting done." It was good to feel solidarity. Too much is coming at me every day in formats that make delivery of information so easy and staying on top of it so hard.

I have an abundance of unanswered texts, lost passwords, partially executed email organization systems, and documents without folders. A tee-shirt says, "I have too many tabs open." Exactly.

The problem isn't that I fail to get it all done (though that's true), but that I equate my fundamental worth with my ability to stay on top of it all. I sometimes feel like I'm a bad robot instead of a beloved human.

Here's what I said to the council: "I don't think Jesus called us into the life of discipleship so we can feel bad about what didn't get done. Jesus called us so we can give and receive divine love."

We have an excellent council. We got through our agenda. At the end of the meeting, something unusual happened. We stayed on Zoom and chatted. It was spontaneous and relaxed, not our normal rush to get onto the next thing.

For those few minutes, we weren't people who sit behind screens ticking through information and accomplishing tasks. We were just people who like each other. We were just people, beloved of God.

Sleep well world. God holds you.

February 15, 2021
Day 338

In my Transfiguration sermon, I asked, "How do you meet Jesus?" Jesus doesn't usually come with bright lights and a voice from God saying, "Here he is." He mostly comes in forms that are easy to miss. He shows up in neighbors and children and anyone in need.

"Just as you did to the least of these . . . you did to me " (Matt 25:40)

I fear I've let the insurrection and impeachment hog the spotlight of my attention lately. That's not to say I think people of faith should ignore these things. Quite the opposite. We are called to pay attention when people are hurt and terrorized, especially when God's name is invoked as a champion of destruction rather than Prince of Peace.

But rather than waiting for a glorious show of Christ's power, I'm ready to come down off of all the mountains for a while. I want to focus my attention on people living in the shadow and the valley, where so much of life is lived. I will meet Jesus every single day there.

Sleep well world. God holds you.

February 16, 2021
Day 339

Shrove Tuesday.

Our church usually has a pancake dinner on this night. I clearly remember last year's. I gobbled up my kids' half-eaten chocolate chip pancakes, swimming in syrup and gooey from deflated whipped cream.

I can recall which kids in the youth group led the burning of the palms. I can picture the exact moment when I saw two newcomers strike up a conversation and thought, *Hmm, that makes sense.* They're now married.

I bounced between long-time members, neighbors who'd come for the first time, the Boy Scout troop, the kids' craft table, and the youth cooking in the kitchen.

I miss being with people in that church-y way, especially tonight. I miss the Fellowship Hall tables that don't fold quite as easily as you think they will, and the vacuum cleaner that never really works. A few people cheerfully put away the dishes while everyone else trickles out. I miss it. May I never take such nights for granted again.

Sleep well world. God holds you.

February 17, 2021
Day 340

Ash Wednesday.

Remember you are dust and to dust you shall return.

An ashed cross on my forehead usually reminds me of death and sin. This year, it reminded me of creation instead.

Adam was made from dust. Humility—from the Latin word for *ground*, or *dustiness*—is the proper stance of one who wants to be remade.

"Create in me a clean heart O God," begged David. "Renew a right spirit . . . restore me to the joy of your salvation." (Ps 51:10–12)

God creates.

I beg for renewed harmony in Eden, restored partnerships between people, and a way through all the wilderness that stretches ahead.

Into the dust of our diminishment and the ash heap of our shame, God's living spirit still breathes. We will be recreated.

These ashes don't just signify death. They remind me that God can make and remake anything. They are the building blocks of the new life to come.

Sleep well world. God holds you.

February 18, 2021
Day 341

Do not wish these days away. That's what I tell myself when I am exasperated with the demands of being a pastor and mother.

This week it has been hard to be both. With the snow day and the holiday, too often I needed to work while also caring for my kids.

I wrote Ash Wednesday reflections with my daughters bouncing on the couch next to me. I participated in a meeting about COVID-related rental assistance with my camera off because I was also building a Lego bakery. The back of my computer is covered with stickers they put on while I was doing pastoral care by email. I didn't even notice they were doing it.

It's helpful for me to remember that I'd be struggling with this even without COVID. I love hands-on mothering. And I love being a pastor. I would gladly throw my whole life into both callings. It's impossible to do both at the exact same time. COVID has intensified a dynamic that was already there.

So I do what pandemic parents have been doing for almost a year. I toggle back and forth and thank God that we have any childcare at all. (We have a fabulous nanny for twenty hours a week). I try to appreciate a husband who is a full partner in it all.

Yes, I am depleted and frazzled, but I am also aware that this exhaustion comes from having too much of what is good.

Someday, possibly soon, the kids will be in school and daycare full time. The house will be quieter and cleaner. I will sleep more and have more sustained focus as a pastor. I will be glad for those days, but I will miss the closeness of all of us under one roof.

I wish for an end to all the devastations of the coronavirus, of course. But I do not wish these days away.

Sleep well world. God holds you.

February 21, 2021
Day 344

Our furnace went out last night. I cycled through panic, shame, and overwhelmedness. Then I pulled it together, said a quick prayer, and reached out. I contacted neighbors and friends, got referrals and was offered a place to crash. Quickly, we were fine. It was fixed in three hours, and we could cover the cost.

It drove home the message of the sermon on the Good Samaritan I myself had written for this morning.

We all need mercy. We all need grace.

I'd written the sermon, but still it surprised me to discover how quickly I felt in the ditch, powerless to help myself and utterly dependent.

I think of the people in Texas, suffering from climate disaster and literally powerless. I think of the five hundred thousand people who have died from COVID-19 in the U.S. in a year. I think of people who live with the constant threat of racism. There is just so much hurt.

The Good Samaritan story shows how to rebuild trust in a society of injured people. Generosity. Courage. New community. Staying with it for the long haul. Doing away with the myth of independence.

In my sermon I quoted Rev. Howard Thurman:

> However strong we may be or think we are, we are
> constantly leaning on others. However self-sufficient we
> are, our strength is always being supplied by others
> unknown to us whose paths led them down our street

or by our house at the moment that we needed the light they could give.[7]

I am grateful for heat and neighbors, for mercy and grace. I am praying for all those who are in the ditch of despair tonight. May you receive the care you need, and then some.

Sleep well world. God holds you.

February 22, 2021
Day 345

Kindergarten.

"Start children off on the way they should go and when they're old they will not turn from it," says Proverbs 22:6.

Tomorrow our daughter will walk through the doors of her elementary school for the first time. She's headed to in-person kindergarten at last. Two days a week. Fewer than ten kids in the class. Masks mandatory. Desks marked off with tape on the floor in the shape of houses. No toys. No circle time. No playground. It's not typical kindergarten, but she's going.

She's ready, and so am I. I'm thrilled for her to be off a computer and relating to live people.

I'm worried about what the pandemic has done to kids. The screen time. The anxiety. The lack of socialization. Our teachers have been going to heroic lengths, and thanks to their undaunted patience and good cheer, it hasn't all been bad. But it also hasn't all been good. Not for us. Not for anyone.

My little girl has finally filled the rainbow backpack she picked out in September. Her clothes are laid out—a new first-day-of-school outfit because she outgrew the original.

She gets to go to school tomorrow and meet these teachers we already love. She'll laugh with the friends she's only seen online. She finally gets to start.

Sleep well world. God holds you.

February 23, 2021
Day 346

Tomorrow I'll lead the first of five sessions of spiritual discernment for the church called "How then shall we live?" I'm excited about it.

I didn't want to rush back into post-pandemic life without taking time to reflect on what has happened. I don't want to go back to normal unless normal was good

We have a great opportunity to lay down new tracks right now, and I think it only happens if we do it intentionally and invite the Spirit to direct us.

So, spiritual discernment with my church.

Scripture and prayer. Community and accountability. A handful of people becoming open to the Spirit, for the care and redemption of the world.

Sleep well world. God holds you.

February 24, 2021
Day 347

Psalm Day.

This morning I passed a neighbor on my walk. We reflexively kept distance as we chatted. Later at the schoolyard, I saw a church member. Same story. Keep distance. Mask up. This has been the social contract in the pandemic, at least for most people I know. You keep me safe. I keep you safe. That's how we survive.

Even without COVID-19, many people in our society constantly navigate potential threats. The pandemic has driven home to me just how stressful it is. We're not wired to make life or death calculations every day.

When I'm stressed, I chafe if someone tells me to relax. But I relax when someone creates an environment in which I am fundamentally safe.

Psalm 122:8–9 says:

> For the sake of my relatives and friends
> I will say, "Peace be within you."
> For the sake of the house of the Lord our God,
> I will seek your good.

My peace is wrapped up in your peace. We can only seek the good if we seek it for each other.

Sleep well world. God holds you.

February 25, 2021
Day 348

We're tip-toeing the kids back into society. Tonight I took them to ride the escalators at a nearby strip mall and shop for some food staples. Our kids love escalators. They've hardly been on one all year, so it was a real thrill to ride three times in a row. And who needs an aquarium when the seafood section of the grocery store has live lobsters?

Ridiculously simple moments are now sources of great fun. That's partly because it's been so long since we've done them, but it's also because I approach them as if they're the destination. I let the kids take time tonight. No rushing. We visited the lobster cage five times.

Yesterday, the church discernment group focused on time. My relationship with time is marked by a sense of scarcity. I generally feel like there's not enough of it.

Pandemic life has, at times, made time seem even more scarce. At other times, however, time has been expansive. With little to do and nowhere to go, there have been more hours where I can fully engage with the moment at hand.

"Give us this day our daily bread," says the Lord's Prayer. (Matt 6:11) I pray this prayer almost every day of my life. I've only recently discovered that this prayer asks God to help us make peace with time.

Today, daily bread looks like escalators and lobsters and kids who think they just had one of the best nights of their lives.

Sleep well world. God holds you.

March 1, 2021
Day 352

Lament.

I lived in a rural village in the country of Malawi as a Peace Corps Volunteer in the late 1990s. There, I experienced wailing. When someone died, the community would bawl and ululate loudly for hours. You could hear the grief-stricken sound from far away. Mourners would gather to join the cry.

For some, it had little to do with a natural expression of grief. It was more performative, like joining a song in progress. Sometimes, to my ears, it seemed artificial, manufactured. But there was great wisdom in it. Taking on an outward, physical manifestation of grief helped people move through it. It helped cue their emotions to be released. It was a catharsis.

Jesus lamented over the city: "Jerusalem Jerusalem, how I have longed to gather you as a hen gathers its chicks." (Matt 23:37)

I feel a strong, physical urge to grieve, out loud and with other people. I have cried plenty of tears through this COVID year and have had days of numbness too. I've even done my own primal screams into the void when I think no one's listening.

Still, I am missing the in-person funeral for the losses of a year. I want to sing mourner's songs and grieve as a body among other bodies. I want to scream and cry and dance and release all this sorrow together so we can make space for what comes next.

How I long to gather you.

Sleep well world. God holds you.

March 2, 2021
Day 353

As we approach what I call the one-year anniversary of the pandemic (March 15), I am reminded of what was happening last year. All the conversations, hand-wringing, and wondering. What activities to cancel? How many groceries to buy?

I remember all the gritty optimism too. We'll get through this together! Wash your hands for twenty seconds and don't touch your face and you'll be fine! We're shutting down now so we can be open by Easter! (We forgot to specify which year).

I find myself resisting the one-year mark. Like a cartoon character who can stick out her heels, grab a door post, and stop forward motion, I want to press pause right now, Day 353. I don't want to pass Go and start another year.

I keep saying, "I can't believe it's almost been a year." I have always heard this sentiment from people grieving loved ones, and now I understand it a bit more. I often suggest that mourners make a plan for the anniversary day, maybe treat themselves to a special dinner or manicure. I advise them to be open to feeling however they feel and not to be ashamed if it is terribly hard nor surprised if it is OK.

I can't press pause. Of course not. What I can do is ask God to make the passage of this particular strip of days on the calendar surprise me with their goodness. I can ask God to replace some of my resistance with openhanded acceptance. Celebration even. We've almost made it a year, folks. Maybe I'll need a good cry and maybe I'll want cake. I think we all deserve some cake.

Sleep well world. God holds you.

March 3, 2021
Day 354

"Speak to my condition, Lord, and change me somewhere inside where it matters."[8]

This line is from a poem "Let Something Essential Happen to Me," by Ted Loder. I used it as the closing prayer tonight for a church discernment group.

Even the most supposedly well-adjusted of us needs a word from the Lord. I believe that to be true at any time, but especially now. Everyone I know is wounded somehow.

Everyone has a condition. Praise be, we also have a God who speaks to us and changes us where it matters.

Sleep well world. God holds you.

March 4, 2021
Day 355

A year ago, when the shutdown started, I quickly realized I'd need help caring for the church.

I went through the directory and made an Excel spreadsheet of everyone who was especially vulnerable. I then gathered church members who had relationships with those people. They became our deacons, named after the group who helped the early church feed widows so the leaders could preach and teach.

Every other week the deacon team has met to talk through how people are doing and what care they could give. They delivered bulletins to folks without printers or computers. They taught some members how to connect online and helped others get food. They dropped off Christmas poinsettias and Valentine's goodie bags. They prayed and generally let people know they weren't alone. The team itself has formed a community. All the while, I've kept notes on that Excel sheet.

Today when we met, the status report for almost everyone changed:

Vaccinated.

I praise God for what that means for these people's lives. Praise also for the people who developed effective vaccines so quickly and for all who helped roll it out. And praise for Peace's deacons. This is church at its best.

Sleep well world. God holds you.

March 7, 2021
Day 358

This is the remembering week.

The restaurant app *Open Table* reminded me that on this night, a year ago, my husband and I went to a fancy dinner, something we rarely do, even pre-pandemic. I remember that night clearly. I ordered butternut squash soup, wine, and something with lobster. I indulged in tiramisu and overpriced coffee for dessert.

Today marked a year since our church gathered in person, in our sanctuary, for Sunday morning worship. I woke up and had a good cry, remembering.

I recall the awkwardness of the receiving line; people wanted to shake hands and then remembered we weren't supposed to shake hands. The retired pastor in our congregation gave me a quick hug, and I gave one back. We knew something big was on the horizon. We had no idea.

I remember these details, stuck in time like a beetle in amber. I have a feeling all week is going to be that way. An astonished, specific, remembering.

My religious tradition places great value in the act of remembering. We tell ancient stories. We recreate Jesus' last supper. We tell one another to remember. Remember that you are dust. Remember your baptism. Remember, Jesus is risen.

Remembering helps us look for God's hand in the past so we can trust God leading us into the future.

Sleep well world. God holds you.

March 8, 2021
Day 359

I met with four other pastors for virtual coffee today. We are Baptist, Presbyterian, Episcopal, Lutheran and United Church of Christ. Our churches are already loosely connected through social ministries, but as pastors, we hardly ever gather.

The agenda today was simple: get to know one another. We shared how we're doing, really. A common theme was the feeling of inadequacy when we've heard how other churches have fared during the pandemic. I've compared myself to those very pastors when I've passed their church signs or eavesdropped on their ministries via social media. But not today. Today it was clear that we are in community, not in competition.

We talked about the challenges ahead, as we brace ourselves for exhaustion-driven bad behavior that could arise as our churches come back together. The hardest days may yet be ahead of us. We talked about how we may be able to help one another.

Community, not competition.

One of the pastors shared this insight: Jesus healed three people from blindness. Once he used spit, once he used his hands, once he used his voice. Three different ways of receiving the gospel probably led to three different styles of ministry, but they all served the same Jesus.

We will meet again in a month. And then again. We will see where it goes. If all that comes is community, it will be plenty.

Sleep well world. God holds you.

March 9, 2021
Day 360

The gears are grinding back on. Our church's renovation team met today, a meeting that was delayed a year. I restarted our kitchen remodel, slated for last spring. An out-of-town friend is coming to town in late April. A church member and I planned a class for June.

We're hardly in full operation—too many people are still getting sick every day—but we're entering a different phase.

I am glad for this new energy. At the same time, I am wary of doing too much. As much as I miss people (and as often I've dreamed of a different kitchen), I don't want to lose the slow pace and somewhat simplified life of the past year. I feel tired just thinking about the kind of schedule I used to keep. I don't want to live that way again.

I like that the post-resurrected Jesus didn't come launching a big program. He didn't have a terribly busy agenda, as far as the Gospels report. He showed up here and there, mostly to his closest friends.

He ate some meals, had good conversations, spoke peace to troubled hearts, and promised the disciples they'd have what they need when they needed it.

Sleep well world. God holds you.

March 10, 2021
Day 361

I have often thought of how much harder this pandemic would have hit my family if we weren't financially secure. For four years, my husband was under-employed. He pieced together jobs as an adjunct professor while looking for full-time, stable work. It was extremely stressful. It took a toll on our relationship. We weren't poor, but we were never at ease. I got really good at doing math in my head.

Six months before the pandemic, he got full-time work. Now both our jobs are relatively secure. This means we've had enough to afford the part-time nanny that felt like a necessity when daycare closed. We can get take-out, give huge tips, and splurge on flowers. We have plenty.

I write all this because tonight it's fairly certain that many Americans will get some economic relief from the American Rescue Plan.

Pastor and economist David Beckmann, retired president of Bread for the World, calls it "the best legislation for poor and near-poor people that Congress has seriously considered in years."[9] I am so glad for all the people who needed a lifeline.

One of the most misused scriptures is Jesus saying, "You will always have the poor with you." (Matt 26:11)

He was speaking directly to Judas, who was stealing from the common purse. He didn't mean, "accept poverty as a part of life." He meant, "poor people will always exist when you don't trust God's abundance enough to share."

I know there's an underbelly to such a massive spending plan. I know taxes may go up, and inflation may rise. But also, it's quite likely that it lifts people out of poverty and sets them on the path to plenty. That's reason to celebrate.

Sleep well world. God holds you.

March 11, 2021
Day 362

A year ago, my biggest fear was that one of my parents would die from COVID-19. I know people who have lost parents to the virus. It's a particular kind of devastation, with no way to gather, no time to process, and no chance to say goodbye.

My parents survived the year, helped by a comfortable place to live, a community of care, good medical advice, personal vigilance, and a fair amount of luck.

Now, not only are they fully vaccinated, but my mother has come to visit. She's sitting next to me on the couch, sharing my blanket, drinking some tea.

I'm going to put down my phone and talk to my mom in person. I thank God that she is here.

Sleep well world. God holds you.

March 14, 2021
Day 365

I wrote a Facebook post the first night our church went virtual.
I had no intention of writing a whole series; I just wanted to
insert a few words of comfort into a world of fear. Then the
next night I did the same. And now it's been a year.

Yesterday, our church hosted a drum circle to commemorate
the pandemic anniversary. Drumming helped us embody our
grief and release it, making space for something new.

The leader taught us a heartbeat rhythm. She invited us to speak
names and losses into the space between beats. *Tha-thump*
(Peggy). *Tha-thump* (Jerry). *Tha-thump*. She said, "Don't worry if
you lose the beat, we've got you."

She and her helper—who happened to be my husband—kept it
going. Some of us novice drummers couldn't name names and
keep a beat at the same time. If we got lost, we could always
find the rhythm again. *Tha-thump. Tha-thump.* I could fully let go,
trusting I was held by that heartbeat.

That's a good description of what writing these posts has come
to mean to me. For a year, I have been nurtured by this
discipline. Most nights, after I put the kids to bed, I've picked
up my phone and thought, *What happened today re: COVID and
what does God have to do with it?* Writing has helped me find my
way to God, day after day. *Tha-thump.* I'm truly grateful for
everyone who has read them. You have been an important
community for me this year. You have held me.

We're in endgame pandemic. It's not over, but shots and
stimulus, spring and sanity do seem to be harbingers of that
elusive time, "after the sickness." After the sickness will bring its

own hard realities, but it will not be the same as what we have just lived through.

I'm going to stop writing soon. A year would be a natural end, but I want to get to Easter. Last year, Easter was our first communion service online. This year, Easter will be our re-gathering as an in-person community, albeit outdoors.

So, three more weeks. To Easter. To resurrection.

Sleep well world. God holds you.

March 15, 2021
Day 366

I wandered around an REI today. I don't quite know why. I just passed it and thought, *I have an extra hour, why not go to REI?*

I haven't had many extra hours in the last year. I also haven't gone into stores for no reason. It reminded me of early outings as a new mother. The time away from the babe was precious, yet I couldn't remember what I used to do.

At REI, I browsed clothes and realized how shabby I've become. I looked at bikes and yearned to be in shape again. I went to an adjacent shoe store and tried on a pair of high-heeled shoes. I didn't recognize myself in the mirror.

This pandemic year has changed me. I'm taking time for mindful conversations and intentional discernment to understand that change.

If today is any indication, I also need to do things that are neither mindful nor intentional. Things like wandering around stores and trying on clothes. It might look like time being wasted.

It is not wasted. Purposeless time is a God-given gift. It's going to help me discover an answer to the question I just now realize I am asking: *Who am I now?*

Sleep well world. God holds you.

March 16, 2021
Day 367

In the beginning, I thought, "We're all in this together" would represent our society's approach to this pandemic. We even put it on our church banner.

It quickly became clear that we weren't in it together, even if the nature of viral spread meant that we were connected in a way we'd never been before. With rare exception, the pandemic inflamed divisions, instead of healing them.

The new version of "we're in this together" is "appeal to unity." Some of these appeals are just fundamentally dishonest, made by people whose actions betray their rhetoric. Even from those who are well-meaning, appeals for unity strike me as incomplete. Unity around what? Unity with whom?

Unity in caring for those immigrants fleeing gang violence and poverty, or unity with those who think they should stay home and live under threat? Unity with people who refuse the vaccine, or unity with those who patiently isolate until their registration number is drawn? Unity with people who think gun rights are unassailable, or unity with people who think we need limits on gun ownership?

Jesus appealed to his disciples to have unity when he was giving his farewell speech. He commanded them to love one another. He wasn't serving up a trite Hallmark-style sentiment. He was telling them that they had to love one another because the world was going to oppose them. The way to keep their Jesus-community alive was to love in the same way that God loved Jesus. Completely. Sacrificially. Joyfully.

I think of Black churches who create powerful unity against the forces that would cause them harm and steal their joy. I think of my denomination's program to accompany migrant minors in need of care. I think of nuns in Myanmar kneeling before police, in unity with protesters. I think of the unity rippling through communities of Asian-American salon workers, hearing news tonight of senseless violence against their sisters and mobilizing to protect themselves.

That's the kind of unity Jesus is talking about when he says, "Love one another." It's the unity that comes to people without worldly power when they are filled with the power that is above all: the love of God.

Sleep well world. God holds you.

March 17, 2021
Day 368

Singing.

Today my brother and my niece both have birthdays. Last year to celebrate, we set up our first-ever family Zoom. With an out of sync rendition of "Happy Birthday," we discovered what every choir has lamented all year: it's impossible to sing together on Zoom.

Our church has done a wonderful job putting together virtual choirs and making music together. When our worship leaders sing the liturgy, I actually feel like I'm singing with them, though I am muted and alone. Still, it's not the same as singing in person.

I like to think that in the future, I will never take the chance to sing with others for granted.

Scripture says, "With gratitude in your hearts, sing psalms, hymns, and spiritual songs to God." (Col 3:16)

I have a mental list of other things I hope to always do with gratitude. Hug. Share a smile. Take in-person communion. Go to concerts. Dance at a wedding. Hear my kids laugh with other kids. The list goes on.

I may walk around the rest of my life amazed at all these beautiful moments. It's more likely, however, that I will soon forget to thank God for such things. I may even get grouchy and sit some songs out.

That's OK. We can't live our lives with intense pressure to make every moment significant.

It will be wonderful if birthday songs and hymns and firepit sing-alongs become so routine that I forget to give thanks every time.

And it will be wonderful if—even years from now—I am blindsided with gratitude for the beautiful, normal, extraordinary thing it is to sing together.

Sleep well world. God holds you.

March 18, 2021
Day 369

As often happens on Thursday night, I am out of words and out of energy. Tomorrow is my Sabbath, the day I tune out of work and tune into my home life. I rest and play with my kids. Sometimes I do laundry too.

Every week, my dear friend sends me a text message on Friday morning. It simply says, "Shabbat shalom," which is a Hebrew greeting that means "a peaceful Sabbath."

It's a habit that she established without us ever discussing it. Come to think of it, I don't know why she started doing it. Now it's been years. I've come to rely on this thoughtful act of faithful friendship. Every time I get the text, I feel like my Sabbath can really start.

This week she sent the message early, tonight instead of tomorrow morning. I think that's a sign to go to bed now.

Shabbat shalom.

Sleep well world. God holds you.

March 22, 2021
Day 373

At some point during the most intense days of the lockdown, someone on social media posted, "Well, at least we don't have to worry about school shootings." I remember thinking, *That's inappropriately flippant and also, true.*

With two mass shootings in less than a week, the particularly American scourge of armed people, almost always white men, terrorizing strangers through senseless gun violence in public settings is back. These weren't school shootings, but it chills me to know that it's just a matter of time.

As a follower of Jesus, I am in favor of laws that restrict access to guns. Truth be told, I fall on the "get rid of the second amendment completely" and "pound them into plowshares" side of the spectrum. Yes, I know. Somehow that's become something radical to say out loud. I never plan to run for office.

Admittedly, the fact that I don't like guns is as much a result of my societal privilege as it is of my religion. I understand that many people find safety in gun ownership that I've never needed. Also, hunters need to hunt.

But I truly don't understand why it's debatable to make sure someone isn't severely mentally ill, or suicidal, before issuing a gun. I don't understand why a country that wants people to live in freedom (from fear, from terror) wouldn't want to limit the type or quantity of guns that one person can own.

With all things, I try to ask myself, *What would Jesus say about this?* His lament from the Palm Sunday entry into Jerusalem comes to mind: "If you, even you, had only known on this day what would bring you peace – but now it is hidden from your eyes." (Luke 19:42)

In the case of guns it seems clear. The Prince of Peace—the one who told his defender to put away the sword when the soldiers came to arrest him; the one whose parting commandment was to love—would be grieved about our collective unwillingness to stop unchecked gun violence from wreaking havoc on our communities.

Sleep well world. God holds you.

March 23, 2021
Day 374

Coronavirus worries are moving to the back of my mind, thanks to successful school reopening, vaccines, and plans for church to re-gather. We even bought plane tickets for a family reunion in late July, so confident am I that travel will be safe. I expect we'll live with masks and low-level risk for at least another year, but the daily fear of coronavirus is receding.

I wish I could report that all that's left now are sunshine and flowers. Indeed, it is a beautiful springtime in Washington, D.C.

But really, other concerns are rushing into that empty space. Racism. Poverty. Refugees. War. Guns. Mental health. Climate.

I have always been someone who is attuned to social issues. But this seems like too much. Is the whole world really just a mess? Has it always been this bad? I wonder if I have become so used to the drama of constant crisis that I have lost the ability to keep everything that's wrong from seeping in all the time.

I think I need to open the floodgates of praise. People praised Jesus as he came into Jerusalem, presumably because they thought he would be victorious. He let them, knowing that even as he went to his own crucifixion, God would have the final word. When threatened leaders told Jesus to calm his people down, Jesus replied that even if there were no people, the stones would shout out in praise.

As my newsfeed fills up with issue after heart-wrenching issue, it is also filling up with moment after moment for God's power to bring life out of death. God will be praised.

Sleep well world. God holds you.

March 24, 2021
Day 375

The word "gentle" leaped off the page at me tonight. We sang it twice in a verse of our evening liturgy:

"Make us shine with gentle justice. . . . Gentle Christ who lights our way."[10]

It was in the Scripture I'd chosen for worship too: "Let your gentleness be known to everyone." (Phil 4:5)

It's got me thinking of images of gentleness. A nurse bathing a patient. A parent putting a blanket on a sleeping child. A potter lifting a new creation off the wheel.

Throughout the pandemic, I've advised many people to "go gentle on yourself." People have said it to me too and—often more important—treated me with gentleness so I didn't have to muster it for myself.

Gentleness is required when things could break, or when things are already broken and in the process of being repaired. Gentleness is an essential characteristic of a caregiver.

It's a beautiful approach to the fragility of this time, when so many people are coming out of caves of isolation into the bright light of social interactions, unsure of where they're damaged, unsure of what comes next.

"Let your gentleness be known to everyone. The Lord is near." (Phil 4:5)

Sleep well world. God holds you.

March 25, 2021
Day 376

In the final session of the Lent discernment group, I asked participants to pick a specific time in the future—say a year—and envision it. They could draw it or write a letter along the lines of, "Dear Sarah, how nice to see that you're still spending lots of time with your kids even though we're done with the coronavirus."

I won't go into the details of my vision, but it surprised me. The quality of life I imagined was less like the years before COVID and more like the year we just lived (minus the constant fear of illness, plus a more just and peaceful world).

I don't think this was just a failure of imagination. The simplicity of the last year brought me a lot of peace, even in the midst of so much ugliness. I miss people, but in some ways I have had more meaningful connections because scheduling was easier and friends were mostly home.

I also have known my call more clearly than ever. Family, church, world. It was the hardest year to be a mother, pastor and citizen, and also the most fulfilling.

The two other times I've done this exercise, the life I imagined turned out to be the life I lived. We shall see.

A song of an ancient prophet flits through my mind: "Write down the vision. Inscribe it on tablets. Ready for a herald to carry it swiftly. Soon very soon it will come to you. Live by faith, Oh righteous one."[11]

Sleep well world. God holds you.

March 28, 2021
Day 379

Palm Sunday.

When my mom visited a few weeks ago, I asked if she wanted to sleep in the kindergarten or the sanctuary. These rooms, formerly known as our home office and our guest bedroom, were repurposed during the pandemic. She chose the kindergarten.

A year ago, Palm Sunday was the last service we held in the church building.

Since then, except for three outdoor services in the fall, I've been Zooming from an altar set up in our guest bedroom.

If all goes as planned, today is the last day I'll lead Sunday worship from my basement sanctuary. I'm glad to move to the next phase (outdoor, in person). Still, I got a bit misty-eyed at the end of an era.

I will miss setting up the space each Sunday—water, wine, bread, candles, flowers—and praying over it all. I will miss the intimacy of knowing the whole church is worshiping in the same way. I will miss listening for my daughters' footsteps clomping down the stairs during the postlude so my little acolytes could blow out the candles.

Liturgical language often mentions "the house" where worship occurs. We heard it twice today:

"We bless you from the house of the Lord." (Ps 118:26)

"For this holy house and all who offer here their worship and praise."[12]

Early in the pandemic, it felt odd to claim my guest bedroom as "the house of the Lord." By now, I know it as a real sanctuary. It is a place where I conducted memorial services and presided over communion. It was a site for transformation and blessing. Many if not all of my parishioners have turned corners of their homes into holy places too. The term "house church" has new meaning.

This week I will rearrange the furniture. It will become a guest bedroom again. But it will also always have a whiff of holiness, even if just in my memory.

Sleep well world. God holds you.

SECTION 6

RESURRECTION
March 29, 2021 – April 5, 2021

"Do not be afraid; I know that you are looking for Jesus who was crucified. He is not here; for he has been raised, as he said." (Matthew 28:5–6)

~~~

"I am asking you to just hold on a little longer, to get vaccinated when you can, so that all of those people that we all love will still be here when this pandemic ends. The nation has so much reason for hope, but right now, I'm scared."

　　—*Dr. Rochelle Walensky, Director of the Centers for Disease Control and Prevention, March 29, 2021*[1]

"CVS Vaccine: Your 1st COVID-19 vaccine dose is on 04/07/2021 at 11:45 AM EDT."

　　—*CVS Pharmacy, text message to the author confirming her first vaccine appointment, April 5, 2021*

March 29, 2021
Day 380

In preparation for my last week of posts, I re-read the whole collection. One overarching theme is the way scripture came alive.

Passages I never understood before suddenly made sense. Passages I thought I knew took on a totally different meaning.

There's still much of scripture I don't understand, but I no longer want to be like Thomas Jefferson and cut out the parts that I don't like. I have been humbled.

I now trust that the most difficult scriptures might illuminate parts of life that I have not yet lived, or history that we haven't gotten to. I also know that sometimes, God speaks when we wrestle with the text.

Today I also read the Maundy Thursday Psalm. It's a confident anthem proclaiming that God can make things right. We read it last year as the pandemic was beginning. We'll read it again in a few days.

I heard it today as I had never heard it before. I felt the relief of survival; the commitment of one who has gone through an ordeal and come through alive; and the deep desire to serve God as a joyful sacrifice of thanksgiving.

I also felt the unnamed sorrow for those who cannot sing this song. For those who didn't make it. For those who called out and didn't get the answer they wanted. For those who literally begged for mercy ("I can't breathe") and then did not get to beg again.

Selections from Psalm 116 (MSG):

> I love God because he listened to me,
> listened as I begged for mercy.
> He listened so intently . . . .
> "Please, God!" I cried out.
> "Save my life!"
> God is gracious—it is he who makes things right,
> our most compassionate God.
> God takes the side of the helpless;
> when I was at the end of my rope, he saved me. . . .
> I'm striding in the presence of God,
> alive in the land of the living!

Sleep well world. God holds you.

March 30, 2021
Day 381

It's Tuesday of Holy Week, and many pastors have already recorded their Easter Sermons, or at least started them.

I have not. In my dozen years of pastorhood, I have learned that I cannot get to Easter until I have gone through the crucifixion.

Lutherans are characterized by something called the theology of the cross. It's the firmly held belief that God is most perfectly, paradoxically, revealed in the crucifixion of Jesus. The resurrection is miraculous, of course, but it's the cross that really shows us what God is made of.

As Martin Luther put it, "A theologian of glory says that evil is good and good is evil. A theologian of the cross says that a thing is what it actually is."[2]

That is one of those things that doesn't make any sense, until it does.

Jesus was killed on a cross after a public trial in which what was being judged was not so much the moral rectitude of one man, but the clash of God's unusual power—God's reign—with the systems that could not handle it.

Holy week is a heck of a time to be conducting the trial over George Floyd's killing. The crucifixion is written all over this one. And so is the truth. George Floyd was murdered. Power in policing needs to change. Let's call a thing what it is, even if the eventual verdict doesn't.

Every time we look at the cross, Christians are trained to see what happens when God meets unjust power. Innocent people suffer, but something else happens too. Jesus shows up. Jesus dies at the hand of our sins. And then the whole thing gets transformed.

Theologians of the cross do not pretend that the world is any rosier than it is. We know ourselves to be first in line as sinners stuck in systems of sin. And yet we also hold that grimness in check. We see the cross as the way to resurrection, we stay humble, and we tell the truth.

Sleep well world. God holds you.

March 31, 2021
Day 382

Citizenship.

I was finally able to register for the vaccine. Whoohoo! Within a month, I expect I will be on my way to becoming a citizen of that new realm: the vaccinated.

Citizenship is a powerful metaphor for vaccinated life. I will be able to go places and be with people freely. If they issue "vaccine passports," I could get one. It reminds me of my yellow WHO card, which enabled me to travel between countries that have vaccine requirements.

Scripture pays a great deal of attention to citizenship. Jesus was not a citizen of Rome but he was tried under its laws. It's debatable if Paul actually was a Roman citizen, but he had at least some of the privileges associated with it. The admonition to "welcome the stranger" is more accurately translated "welcome the foreigner," a.k.a. the non-citizen.

I am a citizen of the United States. This is a weighty piece of identity, especially when citizenship questions like, "Who gets to vote?" and "Who gets protection under the law?" and "Who gets to take refuge here?" beg for response.

The Christian is never just a citizen of a country. She is first and foremost a citizen of the kingdom of God. All other citizenships are subsumed under this identity, including what it means to be vaccinated.

Should only those who are vaccinated be allowed to worship? Attend school? Teach?

What about those who refuse the vaccine? In the kingdom of God, there are no second-class citizens, but there are people who refuse to do what it takes to belong. How is grace extended to them? What is justice?

I will take my shot when it comes. I will be thrilled. But I'll also be aware that I will no longer be in the same category as unvaccinated people. This includes my own children.

I hope that soon we will all be vaccinated—here and around the world. Until then, I hope my status will not cause me to disassociate from people who can't get it, including the global poor. I hope I will remember that we are all citizens of one kingdom, and there is no distinction.

Sleep well world. God holds you.

April 1, 2021
Day 383

"I've been waiting for this!" my four-year-old daughter
exclaimed loudly from her perch on my hip, where I held her as
I started the communion liturgy.

"Shh, everyone can hear us," I said, aware that my Zoom was
not muted. So she whispered it again in my ear, beaming with
joy: "I've been waiting for this!" Afterward I asked her what she
was talking about.

Communion. That's what she was so excited about.

Last Easter, I made the decision to offer communion during
online worship. Starting then, I could have joined my family for
the holy meal. They were usually one floor above me,
worshiping at our dining room table.

Instead, I intentionally chose to worship in a different room for
the whole service and give myself communion.

One reason for this was practical; it's very distracting to preside
over a communion table with wiggly, talkative kids. The main
reason, however, was pastoral. I was convinced that it was right
to do communion online, but I wanted my experience to
confirm that. I thought it was important to be having the same
form of communion that I was asking my people to have, many
of whom were physically alone. I didn't want the image of my
familial communion to make anyone feel even more isolated
than they were.

For a year, I watched the rest of my family take communion
over Zoom. After worship, I'd find their half-full grape juice
bottles and special cups on the kitchen counter as proof of their

participation in the sacrament. I knew we took communion at the same time, but I was never physically with them.

Tonight was the first time in a year I have taken communion from someone else's hands. Tonight was the first time I've given it that way too.

My husband and daughters gathered around the table together. We gave each other bread and wine. My sweet child's joy was spot on.

I've been waiting for this.

Sleep well world. God holds you.

April 5, 2021
Day 387

Easter Monday.

We celebrated Easter with an in-person, outdoor, worship service complete with sweet-smelling lilies, triumphant organ, and rows of people. It was glorious.

It was also extremely windy. There was no chance the paschal candle would stay lit. Tents and bulletins and my Easter hairdo were all blowin' in the wind. Even our heavy, rough-hewn cross got knocked over by a gust. When it crashed to the ground behind me, it broke.

A broken cross seems like the right way to end one season—Lent, coronatime—and begin another.

This past year has been one of intense breakage. Supply chains and systems meant to protect. Beloved bodies. Human hearts. Broken.

People died. Communities were devastated. Some of the fissures may not fully heal in this lifetime. There is much to repair.

Broken and blessed. Broken for you. Jesus broke the bonds of hell, death, sin. Broken works both ways.

Some of what broke needed to go. It broke in order that people may be free. James Cone, in his book *The Cross and the Lynching Tree*, reminds us that before the cross became a symbol of resurrection, it was an instrument of death. He wrote, "The cross can heal and hurt; it can be empowering and liberating but also enslaving and oppressive. There is no one way in which the cross can be interpreted."[3]

And so a broken cross for people who have been isolated and ill, impoverished and afraid. A broken cross for people who have been enslaved and oppressed, damaged and destroyed. A broken cross for coronavirus and racism, mental illness and lies. A broken cross for all the ways incarnated evil tries to tell us that the twin powers of death and sin are winning. Take it away, I say. Break it over your knee. It is Easter now. It has no more power.

The cross broke behind me. That which was in front of me stood firm: the welcome table, set with plenty of bread and wine. And the church, the resurrected people of God.

It's Easter. We will worship from the church building from here on out. My child will start four-day a week in-person school in two weeks. I am getting vaccinated in two days. The virus isn't over, but fifty-five weeks ago when I started posting, I said I'd end on Easter, and here we are.

This is my last post. I never intended to do this for so long. I just never stopped. That's because I have loved it. I love the act of writing, of thinking of the right word to convey the truest thing. But more, these posts have brought meaning, community, and God's presence into my life. It has held me. You have held me.

It is a hard thing to stop. I will miss it. But I am exhausted. It is time to sleep and dream, exercise, spend time with my husband, and let a new thing come. I reserve the right to post again from time to time, to develop a new format for "God Holds You," should the spirit blow me in that direction. For now, however, I am done.

It is Easter. I end where I begin, with Jesus' resurrection. Despite all worldly evidence to the contrary, I believe God brings life from death, love from hate, healing from illness, abundance from scarcity, community from isolation, righteousness from injustice, and beauty from ugliness. I believe this with all my being. The cross has no more power. Jesus is risen. Alleluia. Amen.

And so, I'll put us all to bed one more time. Grateful. Tearful. Alive and full of hope.

Sleep well world. God holds you.

~Pastor Sarah

ACKNOWLEDGEMENTS

My biggest thanks go to my husband Ridgeway Addison, who encouraged me to write every night, never resented the time it took, and lovingly read every post. Thanks also to our two kiddos, who are on every page of this book.

Huge thanks to Tiffany Tibbs, my book doula, editor, and dear friend. You believed in this book and picked it up when I was ready to put it down. You made it happen. And thanks to the third person of our friendship trinity, Rachel Bass-Guennewig. You are my friends forever.

Thanks to the rest of my family. To my parents, Michael and Suzanne, for always encouraging your pastor-daughter and giving me a backbone of faith. To my in-laws James, Linda and Heather, for all your love.

To my brother Jason, who edited a rough draft. Your writing inspires me. And to the other "sibs and spice," Margie, Zachary, Anna, Benji, Emily, Rebekah, and Shawn. Your texts, songs, and Zoom check-ins were bright spots on dreary pandemic days.

Thanks to Marge Barrett for adding your voice in the Foreword, and to the rest of the Wholly Writers—Arianne Lehn, Brooke Heerwald Steiner, Lori Raible, and Deborah Lewis. Your friendship and talent have kept me writing and laughing. What a gift we have in one another!

Thanks to two parish administrators, Kris Rinnert and Josh Keiter. Kris faithfully reposted my writing every morning; Josh made sure it wasn't all lost in the cloud. Both were essential.

Thanks to two Peace Lutheran Churches. First, Peace in Alexandria, Virginia, where I served as a pastor throughout the pandemic. Thanks especially to our staff Nadia Fitzcharles,

Paul Sticha, Jim Nice, Adela Peeva, Reena Abu-Taleb, and Sophie Morgan; Council Presidents Norm Philion and Natalie Cain (who gave publishing advice); and tech wizard Andrew Tlusty. I could list every members' name here. I can't think of a better group of people to go through a pandemic with.

And second, Peace in Robbinsdale, Minnesota, the church where I grew up. Through the wonder of Facebook, Pastor Carleton and Zelda Zahn, Dawn VanTassel (RIP), and other early faith influences became part of my "God Holds You" community forty years later. Blest be the ties that bind!

Thanks to Autumn Kendrick for her cover design, and to artists Jill Weddall and Marni Maree for their creative insights. Thanks to Melissa Von Rohr and Matt Heidenry for editing consultation, and to Christian Eriksen for legal advice.

Thanks to Trina and Sarah for caring for our kids so excellently. To Christy Schwengel for cheering me on. And to neighbor Margie, our bonus grandma, for being part of many of these days.

Thanks to the Reverends MaryAnn McKibben Dana, Carmelo Santos, and Jason Micheli for writing early reviews and modeling how to be a pastor, practical theologian, and writer. Thanks also to Reverends Bob Holum, Roy Howard and Brian Erickson, for sharing your wisdom so freely. Thanks to my courageous, insightful Bishop, Rev. Leila Ortiz. And thanks to professors at Valparaiso University and Yale Divinity School for teaching me how to write my faith.

Finally, thanks to every person who read a post, shared a prayer, or otherwise became part of the extended web of people reminding one another of God's presence through the pandemic. We held each other. You are too many to name, and I am grateful for every single one of you.

NOTES

Section 1 – Into the Wilderness

1. Peter Wehner, "NIH Director: 'We're on an Exponential Curve,'" *The Atlantic,* March 17, 2020, https://www.theatlantic.com/ideas/archive/2020/03/interview-francis-collins-nih/608221/.

2. "Transcript: Dr. Anthony Fauci discusses coronavirus on 'Face the Nation,' March 15, 2020," Face the Nation, CBS News, https://www.cbsnews.com/news/transcript-dr-anthony-fauci-discusses-coronavirus-on-face-the-nation-march-15-2020/.

3. Desmond Tutu, *Children of God Storybook Bible* (Grand Rapids: Zonderkidz, 2010).

4. Jack Gilbert, "A Brief for the Defense," from *Refusing Heaven: Poems* (New York: Knopf: distributed by Random House, 2005).

5. Jez Alborough, *Hug* (Somerville: Candlewick Press, 2002).

6. Fred Pratt Green, "God Is Here," Hope Publishing Company, 1979. Published in *Evangelical Lutheran Worship*, Hymn #526. All rights reserved. Used by permission.

7. Paul Sticha, "His Steadfast Love," 2020.

8. Dr. Seuss, *The Lorax* (New York: Random House, 1971).

9. Peter Spier and Jacobus Revius, *Noah's Ark* (Garden City, N.Y: Doubleday, 1977).

10. Sam Nzima, Talk at the Apartheid Museum in Johannesburg South Africa, Spring 2007.

Section 2 – Looking in on Pentecost: The World's on Fire

1. Editorial Board Star Tribune, "'Please, Please, Please, I Can't Breathe,'" *Star Tribune*, May 26, 2020, https://www.startribune.com/please-please-please-i-can-t-breathe/570783012/.

2. John Lewis, "Together, You Can Redeem the Soul of Our Nation," *The New York Times,* July 30, 2020, https://www.nytimes.com/2020/07/30/opinion/john-lewis-civil-rights-america.html.

3. Marriage Liturgy, Prayers of Intercession, *Evangelical Lutheran Worship Leaders Edition,* (Minneapolis: Augsburg Fortress, 2006), page 684.

4. Compline Liturgy, *Evangelical Lutheran Worship,* (Minneapolis: Augsburg Fortress, 2006), page 320.

5. Ibid., page 327.

6. It is unclear who said this first. I encountered it in this quote:

"There's a Chinese saying. 'When is the best time to plant a tree? Twenty years ago.' The Chinese engineer smiles. 'Good one. When is the next best time?' 'Now.'"

Richard Powers, *The Overstory* (New York: W. W. Norton & Company, 2018), page 30.

7. Gustaf Wingren, *Luther on Vocation,* trans. Carl Rasmussen (Eugene, Oregon: Wipf & Stock, 1957), page 10.

8. Compline Liturgy, *Evangelical Lutheran Worship* (Minneapolis: Augsburg Fortress, 2006), page 325.

9. Sermon preached by Reverend Angela Shannon, June 17, 2020. Used by permission.

10. Ibid.

11. Gaby Galvin, "Study: Lockdowns, Restrictions Averted 60 Million Coronavirus Infections in U.S.," *U.S. News and World Report,* June 8, 2020, https://www.usnews.com/news/healthiest-communities/articles/2020-06-08/restrictions-averted-60-million-coronavirus-infections-in-us-study-says.

12. Sandra Boynton, *The Going to Bed Book, Boynton Board Books* (New York: Little Simon, 2012).

13. Martin Luther, "Luther's Lecture on Romans," found in *Luther's Works, vol. 25* (St. Louis: Concordia Publishing House, 1972), page 345.

14. Mary Louise Pringle, "Light Dawns on a Weary World," GIA Publications, 2002. Published in *Evangelical Lutheran Worship,* Hymn #726. Used by permission.

15. Priscilla Alvarez, "Nearly 75% of Detainees at US Immigration Facility in Virginia Have Coronavirus," *CNN Politics,* July 23, 2020, https://edition.cnn.com/2020/07/23/politics/immigration-ice-detention-coronavirus-farmville/index.html.

16. "William Wilberforce," Wikipedia, accessed July 22, 2020, https://en.wikipedia.org/wiki/William_Wilberforce.

17. John C. Ylvisaker, "Borning Cry," 1985. Published in *Evangelical Lutheran Worship*, Hymn #732.

18. Marty Haugen, "All Are Welcome," GIA Publications, 1994. Published in *Evangelical Lutheran Worship*, Hymn #641. Used by permission.

19. Ibid.

20. John Lewis, "Together, You Can Redeem the Soul of Our Nation," *The New York Times,* July 30, 2020, https://www.nytimes.com/2020/07/30/opinion/john-lewis-civil-rights-america.html.

21. Ibid.

Section 3 – Orienting Toward Hope

1. Teacher, personal communication, October 20, 2020.

2. Jack Healy, Lucy Tompkins, and Audra D. S. Burch, "'A Shot of Hope': What the Vaccine is Like for Frontline Doctors and Nurses," *The New York Times*, December 14, 2020, https://www.nytimes.com/2020/12/14/us/coronavirus-vaccine-doctors-nurses.html.

3. Chimamanda Ngozi Adichie. "The Danger of a Single Story." Filmed July 2009 in Oxford, England. TEDGlobal video, 18:33. https://www.ted.com/talks/chimamanda_ngozi_adichie_the_danger_of_a_single_story/transcript.

4. Bob Woodward, *Rage* (New York: Simon & Schuster, 2020).

5. Eucharistic Prayer xi, *Evangelical Lutheran Worship* (Minneapolis: Augsburg Fortress, 2006), page 69.

6. Confession, option A, *Evangelical Lutheran Worship* (Minneapolis: Augsburg Fortress, 2006), page 95.

7. *Common English Study Bible*, ed. Joel Green (Nashville: Common English Bible, 2013).

8. Compline Liturgy, *Evangelical Lutheran Worship* (Minneapolis: Augsburg Fortress, 2006), page 326.

9. Eric Metaxas, *Bonhoeffer: Pastor, Martyr, Prophet, Spy* (Nashville: Thomas Nelson, 2011).

10. Mike Pence, "Transcript: Mike Pence's RNC Speech," *CNN*, August 26, 2020, https://www.cnn.com/2020/08/26/politics/mike-pence-speech-transcript/index.html.

11. *Madam Secretary*, season 6, episode 2, "The Strike Zone," directed by Felix Alcala, written by Joy Gregory, aired October 13, 2019, on CBS.

12. "If you believe what you like in the Gospels, and reject what you don't like, it is not the Gospel you believe in but yourself." Commonly attributed to St. Augustine, source unknown.

13. Dietrich Bonhoeffer, *Life Together,* trans. John Doberstein (San Francisco: Harper Collins, 1954), pages 17-18.

14. Martin Luther, "A Mighty Fortress Is Our God," Published in *Evangelical Lutheran Worship*. Hymn #504. Used by permission.

15. Dietrich Bonhoeffer, "By Gracious Powers," translated by Fred Pratt Green, Hope Publishing Company, 1974. Published in *Evangelical Lutheran Worship*. Hymn #626. All rights reserved. Used by permission.

16. "Anyhow," by Amy Ray, *Goodnight Tender*, Daemon Records, 2014.

17. Thomas Troeger, "The Dream Isaiah Saw," poem written in 1994, assigned to Oxford University Press, 2010.

18. Barbara Brown Taylor, *Learning to Walk in the Dark* (New York: HarperOne, 2014).

19. Vespers Liturgy, *Evangelical Lutheran Worship* (Minneapolis: Augsburg Fortress, 2006), page 317.

20. Madeleine L'Engle, *A Wrinkle in Time* (New York: Ariel Books / Farrar, Straus and Cudahy, 1962).

Section 4 – Three Weeks of Revelation

1. Laurel Wamsley, "Obama: 'A Moment of Great Dishonor and Shame for Our Nation'—But Not a Surprise," *NPR*, January 6, 2021, https://www.npr.org/sections/congress-electoral-college-tally-live-updates/2021/01/06/954218662/obama-a-moment-of-great-dishonor-and-shame-for-our-nation-but-not-a-surprise.

2. 117th Congress (2021-2022), H.Res.24–Impeaching Donald John Trump, President of the United States, for high crimes

and misdemeanors, engrossed in House 01/13/2021, https://www.congress.gov/bill/117th-congress/house-resolution/24/text/eh.

3. Amanda Gorman, "The Hill We Climb," printed in "Read: Youth Poet Laureate Amanda Gorman's Inaugural Poem," *CNN*, January 20, 2021, https://www.cnn.com/2021/01/20/politics/amanda-gorman-inaugural-poem-transcript/index.html.

4. "A Change Is Gonna Come," by Sam Cooke, *Ain't That Good News*, RCA Victor, 1964.

5. Audra D. S. Burch, John Eligon, and Michael Wines, "The Words of Martin Luther King Jr. Reverberate in a Tumultuous Time," *The New York Times*, January 18, 2021, https://www.nytimes.com/2021/01/18/us/martin-luther-king-words-protests.html.

6. "Ring Them Bells," by Bob Dylan, *On Mercy,* Columbia Records, 1989.

7. "632: To Emile Bernard. Arles, Tuesday, 26 June 1888," Vincent Van Gogh, *The Letters*, Van Gogh Museum, accessed January 20, 2021, https://vangoghletters.org/vg/letters/let632/letter.html.

Section 5 – The Last Days of a Long Lent

1. Julie Bosman, "A Ripple Effect of Loss: U.S. Covid Deaths Approach 500,000," *The New York Times*, February 21, 2021, https://www.nytimes.com/2021/02/21/us/coronavirus-deaths-us-half-a-million.html.

2. "Coronavirus One Year Later: Live interview with Scott Gottlieb and Leana Wen," *Washington Post,* March 11, 2021, https://www.washingtonpost.com/washington-post-live/2021/03/11/transcript-coronavirus-one-year-later-with-scott-gottlieb-leana-s-wen/.

3. Giulia Heyward and Brian Ries, "A New Jersey School District Promised to Keep Its Snow Days So Kids Can Just Be Kids," *CNN*, October 29, 2020, https://www.cnn.com/2020/10/29/us/new-jersey-school-district-snow-days-pandemic-trnd/index.html.

4. Wallace Stegner, *Angle of Repose* (New York: Penguin Books, 1971).

5. This phrase comes from the following book: Marcus J. Borg, *Meeting Jesus Again for the First Time: The Historical Jesus & the Heart of Contemporary Faith* (San Francisco: HarperSanFrancisco, 1994).

6. J. Clinton McCann, Jr, "Commentary" in the *Common English Study Bible*, ed. Joel Green (Nashville: Common English Bible, 2013), page 842.

7. Howard Thurman, *Meditations of the Heart* (Boston: Beacon Press, 1999).

8. Ted Loder, "Let Something Essential Happen to Me," in *Guerillas of Grace; Prayers for the Battle* , 20th ed. (Minneapolis, Augsburg Fortress, 2004).

9. David Beckmann, "The best legislation for poor and near-poor people that Congress has seriously considered in years," Facebook, March 4, 2021, https://www.facebook.com/revdavidbeckmann/posts/pfbid02w4r MY3qkJbxP5RQqNfdh3xjxSgVzrMUcTEt4k7yr5C6oVTRhzfrYP LMtg3HH1LDul.

10. Marty Haugen, "Joyous Light of Heavenly Glory," GIA Publications, 1987. Published in *Evangelical Lutheran Worship*, Hymn #561. Used by permission.

11. John W. Arthur, "Climb to the Top of the Highest Mountain," Contemporary Worship, 1972. Published in *Lutheran Book of Worship.*, Canticle #7 (Minneapolis: Augsburg Fortress, 1978).

12. Kyrie, *Evangelical Lutheran Worship* (Minneapolis: Augsburg Fortress, 2006), page 317.

Section 6 – Resurrection

1. Sharon LaFraniere and Sheryl Gay Stolberg, "Biden Pushes Mask Mandate as C.D.C. Director Warns of 'Impending Doom,'" *The New York Times*, March 29, 2021, https://www.nytimes.com/2021/03/29/us/politics/biden-virus-va ccine.html.

2. Martin Luther, "Theses for Heidelberg Disputation," in *Martin Luther: Selections from His Writings*, ed. John Dillenberger (New York: Anchor, 1962), page 503.

3. James Cone, *The Cross and the Lynching Tree* (Maryknoll, New York: Orbis, 2013), page xix

INDEX OF BIBLICAL REFERENCES

ABOUT THE AUTHOR

Sarah S. Scherschligt is the Pastor of Peace Lutheran Church in Alexandria, Virginia. Originally from Minnesota, she lives near Washington, D.C. with her husband and two daughters.

She studied at Valparaiso University, Yale Divinity School, and Pacific Lutheran Theological Seminary. Prior to becoming a pastor, she served in the U.S. Peace Corps (Malawi, '96-98) and worked for Augsburg College's Center for Global Education & Experience in both Minnesota and Namibia. She is an environmental activist and amateur potter. Her writing has appeared in *The Christian Century, The Presbyterian Outlook, BoldCafe,* and *The Washington Post.*

More about Sarah, as well as a reflection guide for *God Holds You,* can be found at www.godholdsyou.com.

~ ~ ~

God Holds You was published in creative collaboration with Tiffany Tibbs, PhD, at Gathering Stories, LLC.

The mission of Gathering Stories is to help individuals tell the stories that matter to them. Gathering Stories provides guidance and support for projects ranging from personal essays to academic work to self-published books. Find out more at www.gatheringstories.org.

Made in the USA
Coppell, TX
01 November 2022